公司治理結構與治理機制研究

基於金融危機、股權分置改革的視角

A Study of Corporate Governance Structure and Governance Mechanisms: Based on the Perspectives of Global Financial Crisis and Split-share Structure Reform

劉春燕、內田交謹 著

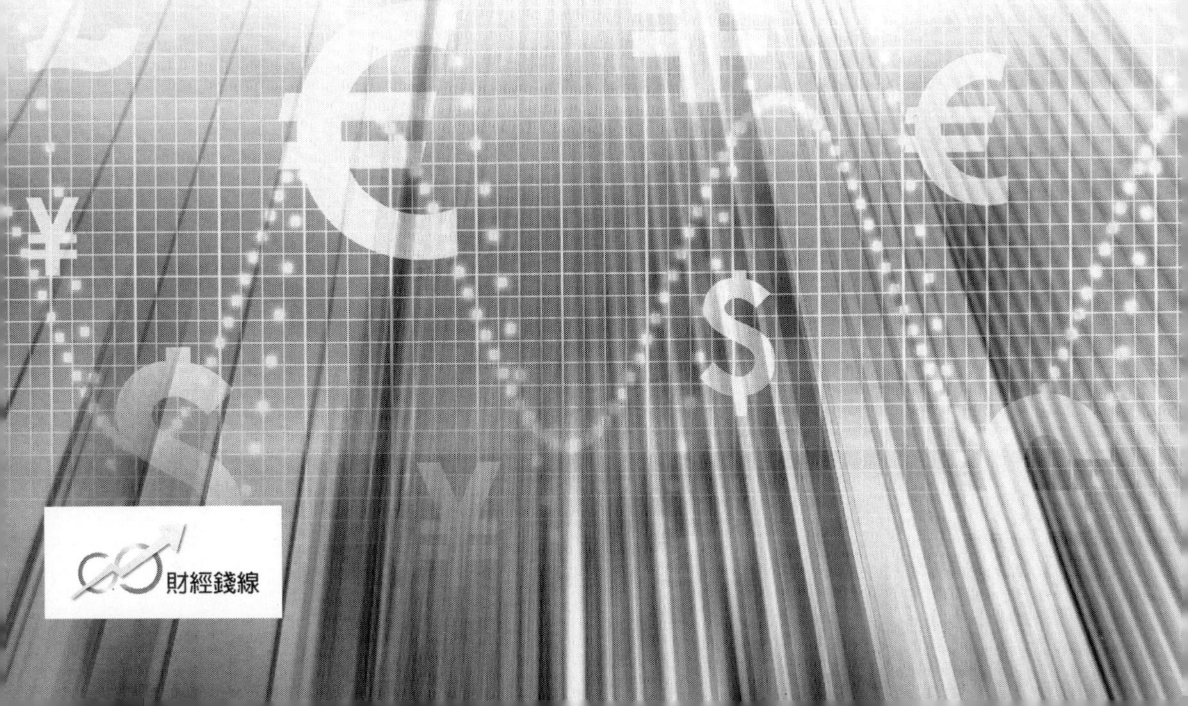

財經錢線

前言

　　隨著中國股票市場對國際投資者的開放和上市公司數量的快速增長,中國公司的委託代理問題以及中國公司的公司治理機制是否能夠有效緩解代理問題受到越來越多學者的關注。中國的公司治理模式來源於西方,但又具有中國特色,公司所有權結構高度集中、股權分置、國家控制、外部治理機制缺乏,容易產生大股東對中小股東利益的侵占問題(即第二類代理問題);中國的經濟環境不同於西方國家,公司治理機制的有效性可能也與其存在差異。

　　近年來,中國政府一直努力改進公司治理水平,以對小股東提供更好的保護。中國證監會2001年公布了《公開發行證券的公司信息披露內容與格式準則》,強化上市公司關鍵財務信息的披露;2001年發布了《關於在上市公司建立獨立董事制度的指導意見》的通知,要求所有上市公司在2003年6月30日前上市公司董事會成員中應當至少包括1/3的獨立董事。為了解決股權分置問題,中國證監會在2005年發布了《關於上市公司股權分置改革的指導意見》,正式啓動股權分置改革。由於大股東持有的往往是非流通股,股權分置改革能增強控股股東最大化股東價值的動力,減少第二類代理問題。本書致力於檢驗中國的公司治理改革是否有效以及中國的公司治理機制是否能夠緩解第二類代理問題。內生性問題一直困擾著公司治理的實證研究,本書的貢獻在於對公司治理內生性問題的控制,選擇的研究方法使研究結果更加可靠、準確,有助於學術界和實務界人士對中國的公司治理和中小股東利益的保護有更好的理解。

　　首先,探究公司治理有效性的一個典型方法是檢驗其對公司業績的影響,本書探究了公司治理機制與公司業績的關係。本書一個明顯

區別於其他研究的地方是採用了2008年全球金融危機期間的數據，全球金融危機事件讓我們在受更少公司治理機制內生性問題影響下重新檢驗公司治理對公司市場業績的影響，也使我們有機會檢驗中國獨特的公司治理結構(國家控股)的另一面。

其次，另一個檢驗公司治理機制有效性的重要方法是考察業績差的公司在高管更替后業績是否改進。本書選擇與高管更替公司在公司規模、帳面市值比、過去股票回報三個維度相近的非高管更替公司作為配對樣本，然后獲得高管更替公司投資者的購買並持有超額收益，以觀察高管更替公司的業績改變。樣本三維匹配的方法可以緩解內生性問題；另外，本書對股權分置改革前后高管更替公司的業績進行了比較，相當於在一個自然實驗中檢驗股票的不可流通性對公司高管更替效果的影響，受到更少內生性問題的影響。該研究有助於理解中國的高管更替是否考慮了中小股東的利益。

最后，根據代理理論，現金股利支付能夠緩解公司內部人與外部投資者之間的代理問題，股利支付行為被認為是對外部投資者利益的保護。但是，有研究文獻發現中國的控股股東由於持有非流通股而偏好現金股利，而中小股東偏好資本利得，控股股東與中小股東之間存在與現金股利支付相關的利益衝突。2005年啓動的股權分置改革使非流通股比例顯著下降，大大降低了公司股權集中度，使我們有機會在遭遇更少內生性問題影響的研究設置下重新檢驗中國公司的所有權結構與現金股利政策之間的關係。該研究有助於理解股權分置改革是否減少了控股股東與中小股東之間的代理衝突。

由於本人時間和水平有限，書中難免有疏漏和不足之處，還請廣大熱心讀者多提寶貴意見。

作　者

摘要

公司治理問題受到學術界和實務界人士的廣泛關注。現有研究關注更多的是西方成熟經濟體的公司治理問題。在新興市場國家，對中小股東權益的法律保護相比成熟經濟體有所欠缺，如何緩解控股股東對中小股東財富的侵占問題是公司治理的一個重要話題。中國公司所有權結構高度集中、存在非流通股，容易產生大股東對中小股東利益的侵占問題。本書運用中國數據研究公司治理機制如何保護中小股東利益的問題。具體來說，本書研究了以下三個方面的問題：(1)在全球金融危機期間公司治理機制對公司市場業績的影響；(2)高管更替後公司市場業績的長期表現；(3)公司現金股利支付與公司所有權結構之間的關係。

已有文獻檢驗了中國公司治理對公司業績的影響，本書在受到更少治理變量內生性問題影響的研究設置下再一次檢驗中國公司治理對公司業績的影響。2007—2009年全球金融危機對單個公司來說是不可預測的，採用全球金融危機期間的數據檢驗治理機制對公司業績的影響可以避免治理變量的內生性問題。研究發現在金融危機前表現差一些的國有企業在金融危機期間反而表現更好了，特別是那些公司所有權結構集中和銀行債務多的國有企業。該結果表明集中的國家所有權緩解了金融危機期間國有企業的財務困境。該研究還發現在控制了各種公司特徵變量後，管理者持股與國有企業金融危機期間的市場業績呈顯著正相關關係，表明管理者持股緩解了國有企業的委託代理問題。最後，還發現聘用有聲譽的會計師事務所擔任審計的公司在全球金融危機期間經歷了更少的市場業績下降。

2005年，為了消除非流通股，中國證監會啟動了股權分置改革，這

為中國的公司治理結構帶來了巨大變化。本書分別探究了股權分置改革前后高管更替公司的市場業績表現，結果表明股權分置改革前高管更替沒有改進公司市場業績，但在股權分置改革完成后，對那些投資者股票回報為負的公司的高管進行更替后，公司股票業績取得了顯著改善。這表明在股權分置改革后，公司控股股東有動力去懲戒市場業績表現極差的公司高管。

　　本書探究了中國上市公司現金股利支付相關的侵占問題，具體研究了股權分置改革前后非流通比例的改變、控股股東持股比例的改變與公司現金股利支付變化的關係。本研究發現現金股利支付在股權分置改革后發生了顯著的下降，且現金股利支付的下降與第一大股東持股比例的下降呈顯著正相關關係，但與非流通股比例的下降無關係。研究結果表明，中國的控股股東對現金股利的偏好歸因於控股股東持有股票固有的流動性不足，而不是股票不可流通本身。

　　本書研究表明，在中國，由於對中小股東保護還不足，加上集中的所有權結構，控股股東的動機非常重要。股權分置改革在一定程度上使控股股東與中小股東的利益協調一致，但是只要控股股東有動機持有充足的股份以達到他們控制公司的目的，控股股東與中小股東之間的利益衝突就不會完全消除。

Abstract

Corporate governance is a topic that has received considerable attention from scholars and practitioners. However, most of the researches hare paid much attention to mature economies in Western countries. An important issue regarding corporate governance is how to mitigate the expropriation of minority shareholders' wealth by controlling shareholders, which is evident in emerging markets that typically have weak legal protection of minority shareholders' rights. China is a typical country in which severe expropriation problems exist due to concentrated corporate ownership structures and the existence of non-publicly tradable shares (NPTS). This book investigates how corporate governance mechanisms protect minority shareholder wealth by using data of China. Specifically, this study explores: ① the influence of corporate governance mechanisms on firm stock performance during the global financial crisis; ② long-term stock performance following top executive turnover; ③ the linkage between cash dividend payment and ownership structure.

Previous studies have examined the effect of Chinese corporate governance on firm performance. This study reexamines this issue in a research environment that is less subject to endogeneity problems. Using data during the global financial crisis, which is an unpredictable event for individual companies, I can avoid endogeneity problems to examine the effect of governance mechanisms on firm performance. The analyses find that state-owned enterprises (SOEs) that performed poorly during the pre-crisis period performed better during the crisis, especially those enterprises that relied on bank debt and had high ownership concentration. This result suggests that state ownership mitigates financial constraints during financial crisis. The analyses also find that managerial ownership is positively associated with the crisis-period performance of SOEs, after controlling for various firm characteristics. This result suggests that managerial ownership mitigates expropriation problems in SOEs. Finally, Chinese firms that adopted a reputable accounting auditor experienced a small reduction in firm value during the global financial crisis.

In 2005, in order to eliminate NPTS, the China Securities Regulatory Commission (CSRC) launched the split-share structure reform program, which substantially changed the Chinese corporate governance structure. I separately examine stock performance following Chief Executive Officer (CEO) turnover before and after the split-share structure reform. The results suggest that CEO turnover before split-share reform caused no significant improvement in stock performance. After split-share reform, however, there is a significant improvement in stock performance following CEO turnover when the firm has exhibited negative prior stock returns. The post-reform result suggests that after split-share reform, controlling shareholders have an incentive to discipline CEOs who show poor stock performance.

Finally, I explore the expropriation problem associated with cash dividend payments in Chinese listed companies. This book investigates the relation between changes in cash dividend payments, non-public tradable shares, and the percentage ownership of the controlling shareholder before and after the split-share structure reform. The analyses find a significant reduction in cash dividends before and after the reform. Importantly, the reduction in cash dividends was significantly related to the reduction in the largest shareholder's ownership; however, it was not significantly associated with the decline in non-publicly tradable shares. These results suggest that Chinese controlling shareholders' preferences for cash dividends are attributable to the inherent illiquidity of their shares rather than the non-tradability of shares.

This study suggests that an incentive of controlling shareholders is particularly important in China, which has weak minority shareholder protection and concentrated ownership structures. This book also finds that the split-share structure reform aligns the interests of controlling and minority shareholders to a certain extent. However, as long as controlling shareholders have an incentive to keep sufficient equity stakes to achieve their goals, the conflict of interests between controlling-minority shareholders will not be eliminated.

Contents

1. Introduction / 1

    1.1 Motivations for the study / 1

      1.1.1 Agency conflicts in corporations / 1

      1.1.2 Corporate governance devices / 3

      1.1.3 Agency conflicts and corporate governance structures in China / 6

    1.2 Objectives of the study / 11

    1.3 Methodology / 14

    1.4 Organization of the book / 16

2. Literature review of corporate governance in China / 17

    2.1 Ownership structure / 17

    2.2 Board of directors / 20

    2.3 CEO duality, CEO compensation, and CEO turnover / 21

    2.4 External governance mechanisms / 24

      2.4.1 Takeover market / 24

      2.4.2 Product market competition / 25

      2.4.3 Legal infrastructure / 25

  2.4.4 Bank monitoring / 26

 2.5 Summary of the literature review and research questions / 27

3. Corporate governance and firm value during the global financial crisis: Evidence from China / 29

 3.1 Introduction / 29

 3.2 Hypotheses / 33

 3.3 Sample selection and data / 37

 3.4 Empirical analyses / 43

  3.4.1 Univariate analyses / 43

  3.4.2 Regression results / 44

 3.5 Additional tests / 50

  3.5.1 Differing definitions of financial crisis periods / 50

  3.5.2 Deletion of outliers / 53

  3.5.3 Pre-crisis period results / 54

 3.6 Conclusions / 57

4. Long-term stock performance following top executive turnover: Evidence from China / 60

 4.1 Introduction / 60

 4.2 Hypotheses / 64

 4.3 Sample selection and data / 67

  4.3.1 Sample selection / 67

  4.3.2 Measure of turnover-related stock performance change / 71

 4.4 Empirical results / 73

  4.4.1 Stock performance following CEO turnover / 73

4.4.2 Cross-sectional determinants of turnover-related change in stock performance / 77

4.5 **Conclusions** / 81

5. **Controlling shareholder, split-share structure reform and cash dividend payments in China** / 83

    5.1 **Introduction** / 83

    5.2 **Hypotheses** / 86

    5.3 **Sample selection and data** / 89

        5.3.1 Sample selection / 89

        5.3.2 Variables / 90

        5.3.3 Data description / 92

    5.4 **Empirical results** / 95

    5.5 **Absolute levels of cash dividends, NPTS, and ownership concentration** / 101

    5.6 **Conclusion** / 104

6. **Conclusion and implications** / 106

References / 109

Appendix / 133

1. Introduction

1.1 Motivations for the study

1.1.1 Agency conflicts in corporations

Corporate governance is a set of mechanisms through which conflicts of interest between stakeholders are mitigated. The most typical conflict of interest in modern corporations is that arising from separation of ownership and control (Berle & Means, 1932). Separation of ownership and control will generate misalignment of interests between managers and shareholders and in turn cause poor firm performance (Alchian & Demsetz, 1972; Fama & Jensen, 1983a; Jensen & Meckling, 1976) (type I agency problem). Jensen (1986, 1989) argued that managers can expropriate dispersed shareholders by diverting corporate resources for perquisites and empire building. From this perspective, corporate governance mechanisms are expected to align the interests of agents (managers) with those of shareholders.

The second conflict of interest exists between debtholders and shareholders (agency problems of debt); debtholders are fixed cash flow claimers who inevitably have different preferences from shareholders who are residual claimants to the firm's income stream. It is well documented that shareholders prefer riskier projects with a higher expected return at the expense of creditors (Jensen & Meckling, 1976), and that shareholders have an incentive to forgo value-increasing projects to transfer wealth from creditors to them (Myers, 1977). Because public creditors anticipate these potential conflicts, borrowers face higher interest rates or must take costly measures to assuage such fears. Indeed, protective covenants are included in many debt agreements to inhibit stockholders from reducing the value of existing creditors' claims on a firm's assets, such as a limitation on the payment of dividends, restrictions on the issuance of additional debt, limitations on the riskiness of the projects undertaken, and so on (Jensen & Meckling, 1976; Myers, 1977; Smith & Warner, 1979).

The third conflict of interests, which has recently received considerable attention from corporate governance researchers, is the expropriation of minority shareholder wealth by controlling shareholders (type II agency problem) (Baek et al., 2006; Claessens et al., 2002; Cronqvist & Nilsson, 2003; Faccio et al., 2001; Fan & Wong, 2002; La Porta et al., 1999; La Porta et al., 2000b; Lemmon & Lins, 2003; Mitton, 2002; Shleifer & Vishny, 1997). Shleifer and Vishny (1997) argue that when controlling shareholders have sufficient equity stakes to control a company, they will pursue private benefits of control that minority shareholders do not share, which results in decreased firm value. La Porta et al. (1999) assert that the central agency problem in large corporations is to restrict expropriation of minority shareholders by controlling shareholders.

It should be noted that different countries face different agency conflicts. When corporate ownership structure is diffused, as is typical for U.S. and UK corporations, agency problems stem mainly from conflicts of interests between outside shareholders and managers who own an insignificant amount of equity in the firm (Jensen & Meckling, 1976). It is well-discussed that in Japan and Germany, major banks monitor managers, and long-term relationships between banks and borrowing companies effectively mitigate the agency costs of debt (Diamond, 1984; Moerland, 1995; Sheard, 1989). In contrast, there are many family-controlled firms or companies with concentrated ownership structures in continental Europe and

East Asian countries, and the type II agency problem is the most prevalent issue in those companies (Claessens et al., 2000; Faccio et al., 2001; Faccio & Lang, 2002).

1.1.2 Corporate governance devices

Corporate governance mechanisms are expected to mitigate agency conflicts. Denis and McConnell (2003) define corporate governance as a set of mechanisms, both institutional and market-based, that induce the self-interested controllers of a company (those that make decisions regarding how the company will be operated, including both managers and controlling shareholders) to make decisions that maximize the value of the company to its owners (the suppliers of capital). Good corporate governance can effectively mitigate agency problems, thus it is vital for shareholder protection and healthy stock markets (Shleifer & Vishny, 1997; Gillan, 2006)

Broadly speaking, researchers generally place corporate governance into two categories: internal and external governance (Hopt et al., 1998; Keasey et al., 1999). Internal governance is constituted primarily of ownership and control, characteristics and composition of the board of directors, and executive compensation and succession; while external governance covers the market for corporate control (the takeover market), production market competition, and the legal systems (Huson et al., 2001; Denis & McConnell, 2003; Gillan, 2006). Some previous studies suggest that significant creditors, like banks, can also provide effective monitoring to firms. (Ahn & Choi, 2009; Diamond, 1984; Hoshi et al., 1991; James, 1987; Lummer & McConnell, 1989; Moerland, 1995; Sheard, 1989).

Among the aforementioned three internal governance mechanisms, ownership structure is crucial to the firm's value maximization. It is reasonable to presume that greater overlap between ownership and control should lead to a reduction in conflicts of interest and, therefore, to higher firm value (Denis & McConnell, 2003; Fama & Jensen, 1983a, 1983b; Jensen & Meckling, 1976). The board of directors is a second mechanism designed to represent shareholders to exercise control and management over a firm, and ensure that the firm's resources are used in the best long-term interest of the shareholders (Jensen & Meckling, 1976; Fama & Jensen 1983a). To effectively perform that function board members should be independent, professional, and have the experience to judge the actions of senior management (Demb & Neubauer, 1992; Beasley, 1996; Rosenstein & Wyatt, 1990; Luis et al., 1987; Yermack, 2006). Managerial compensation and succession is another internal mechanism intended to align the interests of managers with those of shareholders and is one of the top responsibilities assigned to the board of directors. In practice, managerial compensation is designed to be dependent on firm performance, and managers are replaced for poor firm performance (Barro & Barro, 1990; Byers et al., 2008; Coughlan, Schmidt, 1985; Huson et al., 2004; Kang & Shivdasani, 1995; Kaplan, 1994; Warner et al., 1988).

An active market for corporate control is considered essential for the efficient allocation of resources (Jensen & Ruback, 1983; Jensen, 1986; Manne, 1965; Marris, 1963; Martin & McConnell, 1991; Scharfstein, 1988). In the event that a firm fails to institute an effective internal governance system, significant agency costs will be imposed on its shareholders. These costs will in turn be reflected in the firm's relative underperformance or low market valuation. Market participants outside the firm are likely to perceive that as an opportunity to acquire the underperforming firm, replace bad management, and create additional value for the shareholders by improving the operations and governance system (Denis, 2001; Eichholtz & Kok, 2008; Jensen & Ruback, 1983; Jensen, 1986; Manne, 1965; Marris, 1963; Martin & McConnell, 1991).

Competitiveness in the product markets is another external disciplinary mechanism that aligns the interests of shareholders and management. Competition in product markets makes profits more sensitive to the efforts of managers, and makes the possibilities of comparisons between the performances of managers intensified. It also distinguishes superior managerial ability (Cuñat & Guadalupe, 2005; Hart, 1983; Hermalin, 1994; Holmstrom, 1982; Nalebuff & Stiglitz, 1983). Thus, competition makes managers deploy the firm's resources efficiently and productively, resulting in firm productivity/efficiency increases (Alison & Mayes, 1991; Haskel, 1991; Hay & Liu, 1997; Januszewski et al., 2002; Nickell, 1996).

The most basic corporate governance mechanisms exist outside the firm, in the system of laws and regulations that govern the firm (Denis, 2001). Much of the difference in corporate governance systems around the world stems from the differences in the nature of legal obligations managers have towards investors, as well as in the differences in how courts interpret and enforce these obligations (Shleifer & Vishny, 1997). La Porta et al. (1998, 2000a) find that cross-country differences in ownership structure, capital markets, financing, and dividend policies are all related to the degree to which investors are legally protected from expropriation by managers and controlling shareholders. Thus, a country's legal system appears to be a fundamental determinant of how its corporate governance structure evolves.

As mentioned, some previous studies suggest that significant creditors, like banks, can also provide effective monitoring to firms. In general, the purpose of bank monitoring is to reduce a bank's credit risk by preventing the opportunistic behavior of a borrower (moral hazard).[①] Importantly, banks have cost advantages in performing a monitoring function, because (i) banks are delegated the task of costly monitoring of loan contracts, and (ii) banks have informational advantages of depositors (Diamond, 1984; Fama, 1985). In many countries, banks extend their control and monitoring of debtors by directly owning company shares and appointing directors (Gorton & Schmid, 2000; Kaplan & Minton, 1994; Santos & Rumble, 2006). Thus, banks can monitor and discipline borrowers and improve firm performance, at least in developed markets (Gorton & Schmid, 2000; Kang et al., 2000).

[①] Credit risk is the risk that a borrower will fail to repay loans and interest as agreed. It is the most visible risk facing bank managers and one of the primary causes of bank failure.

1.1.3 Agency conflicts and corporate governance structures in China

As China opens its stock market to the international investment community, increasing numbers of international investors are likely to become interested in understanding issues of both agency conflicts in China and whether current corporate governance mechanisms are effective in mitigating agency conflicts. Chinese companies experience special agency problems due to concentrated state ownership and a unique split-share structure, which generate typical type II agency problems. Together with the recent tremendous growth of Chinese firms, this fact has motivated many researchers to investigate Chinese corporate governance (Berkman et al., 2009; Chen et al., 2009; Bai et al., 2004; Jiang et al., 2010; Li, 2010; Li et al., 2007; Liu & Lu, 2007; Qiang, 2003; Qi et al., 2000; Wei & Xiao, 2009; Wei et al., 2005; Yeh et al., 2009; Zou et al., 2008). China has adopted corporate structures that resemble Western corporations. However, Chinese corporate governance has specific features inherited from a socialist background (Fan et al., 2007; Nolan, 1996; Huang & Song, 2005). Since Chinese firms are operating in a context that is different from a Western market economy, the effectiveness of governance mechanisms may differ from that in Western countries (Hoskisson et al., 2000; Tian & Lau, 2001). This subsection presents characteristics of Chinese corporate governance structures.

(1) Highly concentrated ownership structure

Chinese corporations have a highly concentrated ownership structure; usually they have a single dominant shareholder whose ownership far exceeds that of the second largest shareholder (Chen et al., 2009; Cheng et al., 2009; Firth et al., 2006a; Gul et al., 2010; Wang, 2005). As a result of the largest shareholder exerting strong controlling power, Chinese corporate boards typically lack independence. Managers are usually appointed by controlling shareholders and represent the interests of these controlling shareholders. Thus, such managers tend to operate firms for the interests of the controlling shareholders, rather than the interests of minority shareholders. Thus, the exploitation of minority interests by controlling block holders in China's listed corporations is possible.

(2) Split-ownership structure

The shares of listed firms were split into non-publicly tradable shares (NPTS), typically held by controlling shareholders, and publicly tradable shares (PTS) that are usually held by minority shareholders. About two thirds of the shares were non tradable (Fan et al., 2007; Huang et al., 2011; Li, Wang, Cheung & Jiang, 2009; Li et al., 2011; Wei & Xiao, 2009; Yeh et al., 2009).[1] This structure came about because when the idea of setting up a stock market was first proposed in the early 1990s, political leaders were worried that the government would lose control of its important state-owned enterprises (SOEs). Thus, this special and intentional split-ownership structure was implemented to help relieve this concern by maintaining the state as the controlling shareholder in listed firms. Indeed, the holder of non-tradable shares is typically the state. This split-ownership structure prevents controlling shareholders from trading their shares and achieving capital gains; as a result, controlling shareholders have an incentive to obtain benefits through other channels, such as unfair related-party transactions, the supply of corporate loans to controlling shareholders, payments made on behalf of controlling shareholders, loan guarantees made on behalf of controlling shareholders, or tunneling dividends (Berkman et al., 2009; Jiang et al., 2010; Lee & Xiao, 2004; Li, 2010; Zhou & Lv, 2008). These behaviors of controlling shareholders lead to significant private benefits for themselves at the expense of minority shareholders. Zou et al. (2008) point out that the conflict of interest between controlling and minority shareholders was exacerbated in China due to the special split-share ownership structure.

---

[1] Both types of shares have the same cash flow and voting rights.

(3) Existence of state control

As the government (or government agencies) exercises control over listed SOEs as the controlling shareholder, government bodies hold a majority or controlling ownership in many publicly listed companies. As agents of the government, Chinese SOEs have multiple and often conflicting objectives pursued by the state shareholder during their operations (Chang & Wong, 2009; Bai et al., 2000; Bai et al., 2006; Liao, Chen, Jing & Sun, 2009). On the one hand, they need to achieve good performance to ensure the appreciation of state-owned assets. On the other hand, SOEs are subject to the influence and control of the government, which tends to use a firm's resources to promote social and political objectives (e.g. maintain social stability and improve employment). However, minority shareholders who held small shares of listed firms had little ability to monitor listed SOEs and had limited influence over managerial decisions.

(4) Absence of effective external governance mechanisms

The UK and US have an active market for corporate control, which disciplines managers. In China, however, due to the substantial state/controlling shareholding, the hostile takeover market and proxy fights were not well developed. Indeed, prior to the non-tradable shares reform it was almost impossible for investors to gain control of a Chinese listed firm by purchasing tradable shares, as on average only one third of total shares of listed firms were tradable. Moreover, a company could hardly acquire another firm without the state's approval.

Recent studies stress that the legal system is an important factor associated with the development of securities markets and the effectiveness of corporate governance (Allen et al., 2005; Aguilera & Cuervo-Cazurra, 2004; DeFond & Hung, 2004; Dittmar et al., 2003; Durnev & Kim, 2005; Klapper & Love, 2004; La Porta et al., 1997; La Porta et al., 1998; La Porta et al., 2000a; La Porta et al., 2000b). The authors also examine measures of China's legal system and compare them to the average measures of the 49 countries studied in La Porta et al. (1998). They show evidence that almost half of countries in the French-origin subsample, which have the poorest protection, have equal or better measures of creditor and shareholder rights than China does. Regarding law enforcement, only criminal legal action (e.g., actions taken by the Securities Exchange Commission) can be taken against public companies in China, and civil litigation (e.g., shareholder class action lawsuits) against public companies is practically unavailable (Li, 2010).

As mentioned previously, banks play a crucial role in corporate governance for some countries. As the big four state-owned banks that are likely to behave in government interests still dominate the Chinese banking industry, the government serves as both a lender and a borrower, which suggests banks would not provide effective governance to debtholders and shareholders; the state usually sacrifices financial interests in favor of social and political interests (Berger et al., 2009; Firth et al., 2008; Tian & Estrin, 2007).

Overall, Chinese listed firms are highly controlled by government, and there are no effective external governance mechanisms; as a result, controlling shareholders can exert substantial power over listed firms. It is difficult for minority investors to force the management, which is usually appointed by the controlling shareholder, to make decisions in their best interest.

(5) Corporate governance reforms in China

So far, this study has argued that Chinese corporate governance has some special characteristics that are likely to engender type II agency costs. In addition, effective external governance devices (e.g., a market for corporate control and bank monitoring) are almost absent in China. However, the government has introduced several policies to improve the situation.

In 2001, the China Securities Regulatory Commission (CSRC) passed a series of 「Regulation for the Content and Format of Public Firms' Information Disclosure」 to reinforce disclosure of key financial information in listed firms. In order to improve the level of listed firms' corporate governance and offer minority investors better protection, the CSRC issued

「Guidelines for Introducing Independent Directors to the Board of Directors of Listed Companies」in 2001. The guidelines were mandatory and required all listed firms to have at least two independent directors on their boards by 30 June 2002, and at least one-third of the board members had to be independent directors by 30 June 2003. Moreover, the CSRC launched the split-share structure reform program in 2005, with the aim of converting NPTS into PTS (CSRC, 2005). In this program, the CSRC required firms to initiate the reform by the end of 2006. In order to obtain the right to sell their untradeable shares in the future, NPTS holders pay compensations to PTS holders, which is determined through negotiation between tradable and nontradable shareholders. After a company's compensation proposal was accepted, NPTS held by controlling shareholders, were converted to PTS gradually in subsequent few years to mitigate stock price volatility (CSRC, 2005).[①] The conversion of NPTS into PTS is likely to increase controlling shareholders' incentives to maximize shareholder value, which ultimately decreases type II agency conflicts.

As mentioned, Chinese corporate governance has special characteristics that generate type II agency problems. Chinese corporate governance has received increased attention from researchers as type II agency problems have become a central issue in international corporate governance research. It is particularly important to examine whether Chinese controlling shareholders extract minority shareholder wealth to understand type II agency problems. It is also important to examine outcomes of the reforms implemented by the China Securities Regulatory Commission (CSRC) to understand effective governance devices that mitigate type II agency problems. Overall, recent data of China offer me a rich research environment on type II agency

---

[①] After a company's reform proposal is approved, the owners of the formerly non-tradable shares must wait 12 months before selling any shares. Moreover, immediately following the lockup, nontradable shareholders who possessed more than 5 per cent of the company's shares were prohibited from trading on the open market for more than 5 per cent (10 per cent) of the company's shares within 12 months (24 months) (CSRC, 2005).

problems and corporate governance.

1.2　Objectives of the study

The objectives of the study are to examine: ① whether Chinese unique corporate governance structures generate type II agency conflicts; ② whether Chinese corporate governance mechanisms contribute to reducing agency problems; ③ whether the split-share structure reform decreases the agency problem. These analyses are likely to contribute to our understanding of type II agency problems. An in-depth understanding of the issues will also help policymakers consider effective regulations on corporate governance. Although many researches address the issues, this study is distinctive in adopting the sample period and methodology, which suffer less from endogeneity problems.

As a typical method of exploring the effectiveness of corporate governance mechanisms is to examine their effects on firm performance, this study will address this issue in China. This research can shed light on whether Chinese corporate governance mechanisms reduce or generate agency problems. Another important method of exploring the effectiveness of corporate governance mechanisms is to examine whether top management is replaced when firm performance is poor, and whether the firm's performance improves after turnover. In China, the unique split-share structure is likely to engender divergence of interests between untradable shareholders (controlling shareholders) and tradable shareholders (minority shareholders) associated with stock performance. However, the split-share structure reform tends to align controlling and minority shareholders' interests in terms of stock price. Therefore, this book intends to examine stock performance improvement following Chief Executive Officer (CEO) turnover separately for firms experiencing turnover before and after split-share structure reform, which can provide insight into whether CEO turnover protects minority shareholders' interests and whether the split-share structure reform decreases the type II agency problem in China's firms. As dividend behavior has typically been used in the literature as the outcome of corporate governance, this book also pays attention to dividend policy in China's firms (La Porta et al., 2000b; Faccio et al., 2001). It is well documented that in China, cash dividend payout reflects the preference of controlling shareholders who held untradable shares, and cash dividends exacerbate the agency problem between controlling shareholders and outside investors rather than mitigate it. This book also intends to address this issue, which can help us understand type II agency problems in China.

Specifically, this study explores the following questions:

What is the relationship between corporate governance mechanisms and firm performance?

If the unique characteristics of Chinese corporate governance engender type II agency conflicts, the characteristics should be associated with poor firm performance. On the other hand, if Chinese corporate governance mechanisms effectively mitigate the problem, the governance mechanisms will have a positive effect on firm performance. A distinctive feature of this study is that it uses data from the global financial crisis. The global financial crisis gives us an opportunity to re-examine the effect of corporate governance on firm stock performance in a research environment subject less to the endogeneity problem of corporate governance mechanisms. It also enables us to examine a different aspect of unique Chinese corporate governance structure (state control).

Does stock performance following top management turnover improve?

A primary outcome of corporate governance is identifying and terminating poorly performing CEOs. Such governance is used to align a manager's incentives with firm performance. If turnover of top management is motivated by a desire to correct poor firm performance in Chinese listed firms, improvements in stock performance should be observed subsequent to the turnover.

These characteristics of Chinese-listed firms imply that controlling shareholders of Chinese listed firms may be less concerned with stock performance in the assessment of managerial performance. However, it is likely that, after completion of the split-share structure reform, firms are inclined to discipline CEOs on the basis of stock performance. As outside (minority) shareholders' wealth depends directly on stock performance, it is important to explore whether stock performance improves following top management turnover among China's listed firms. This analysis can offer insights on whether CEO turnovers are determined in minority shareholders' interests. It should also be stressed that the investigation offers a natural experiment on whether non-tradability of shares generates the turnover of CEOs who have distorted incentives from shareholder value maximization.

How is cash dividend payment related to ownership structure?

Based on agency theory, cash dividend payout is a mechanism used to reduce agency problems between corporate insiders, such as managers and controlling shareholders, and outside investors (La Porta et al., 2000b; Faccio et al., 2001). However, previous studies show that Chinese controlling shareholders prefer cash dividends due to the untradability of their shares, while minority shareholders (outsider investors) prefer capital gain because of the tax advantage of capital gain (Cheng et al., 2009; Huang et al., 2011; Lin et al., 2010; Wei & Xiao, 2009). Therefore, a conflict of interest exists between controlling and minority shareholders associated with cash dividends in China's listed firms. The split-share structure reform, which resulted in a substantial reduction in the proportion of NPTS, gives us an opportunity to re-examine the relation between ownership structure and dividend policy in China in a research setting suffering less from the endogeneity problem. The analysis also provides insights into whether the split-share structure reform decreases agency conflicts between controlling and minority shareholders.

1.3 Methodology

Empirical studies in corporate governance seek to understand the effectiveness of various governance mechanisms and their potential impact on firm value. A problem that commonly annoys empirical corporate governance researchers is the endogeneity problem (Himmelberg et al., 1999).

This problem manifests either as a spurious correlation between the dependent and explanatory variables or as reverse causality in regression models. In the first instance, spurious correlation confounds empirical results when no economic causal relation truly exists between the dependent and independent variables, but some unobserved variable is related to both the dependent variable and the independent variable. Empirically, we would observe a significant relation in our regression model between the dependent and independent variables, which however, is spurious and not a causal relation. On the other hand, reverse causality taints regression results when we find a significant relation between the dependent and independent variables but there is no clarity on the direction of causality. Therefore, empirical results are likely to be biased and inconsistent without testing and effectively controlling for the potential endogeneity of explanatory variables.

As mentioned previously, this study mitigates this issue by conducting empirical analysis under a research setting subject to less of an endogeneity problem. In Chapter 3, the study chooses the financial crisis period to examine the effects of corporate governance on firm performance in Chinese listed firms. As a financial crisis is a sudden, unpredictable event, it is extremely difficult for firms to adjust their optimal corporate governance structures in response to a future financial crisis. Thus we can treat corporate governance structures as exogenous variables that explain firm performance during a subsequent financial crisis. The study, therefore, adopts corporate governance data at a time before the financial crisis to mitigate the likelihood that our results are affected by the possibility that different firms may endogenously and optimally choose corporate governance practices.

In Chapter 4, in order to measure CEO turnover-related long-term stock performance change subsequent to managerial turnover in China's firms, I matched CEO turnover firms with a non-turnover benchmark firm in three dimensions: size, B/M, and past return, and then subtracted the buy-and-hold returns of the matched firm from the corresponding holding period return for the CEO turnover firm. Thus, I obtained the abnormal buy-and-hold return (*BHAR*) of the sample company. The three-dimensional matching method can yield well-specified test statistics (Lyon et al., 1999), and also can control the price momentum effect (Carhart, 1997; Jegadeesh & Titman, 1993) as well as the effect of mean reversion of the stock performance (Balvers et al., 2000; Campbell & Shiller, 1988). Therefore, our method can provide useful insights in determining whether the turnover of CEOs is truly a value-increasing activity in terms of stock performance in Chinese listed firms. In addition, this study compares the turnover-related performance changes between pre- and post-split share structure reform periods. Split-share structure reform, which is launched by the state, is an exogenous shock for individual firms. This analysis provides me an opportunity to investigate the effect of share non-tradability on the effectiveness of CEO turnover in an environment that is less subject to endogeneity problems.

Chapter 5 also takes advantage of the split-share structure reform to explore the relationship between cash dividend preference and ownership structure in Chinese listed firms. We can treat change of ownership structures associated with split-share structure reform as exogenous variables that explain change in cash dividend payout before and after the reform. Therefore, our documented relation between change in ownership structure and change in cash dividend is attributable to the exogenous reduction in NPTS (ownership concentration), not to the change in cash dividend payments.

1.4 Organization of the book

The rest of the book is divided into the following five chapters.

The next section, Chapter 2, gives an overview of corporate governance literatures in China.

Chapter 3 re-examines how Chinese corporate governance mechanisms affected firm performance in China during the global financial crisis.

Chapter 4 explores stock performance improvement subsequent to CEO turnover in Chinese listed firms during the period 2001—2007.

Chapter 5 takes advantage of the split-share reform to explore the relation between cash dividend payments and ownership structure in Chinese listed companies.

Finally, Chapter 6 concludes and discusses the implications of the study.

2. Literature review of corporate governance in China

2.1 Ownership structure

Existing literatures show that ownership in public firms outside the United States and the United Kingdom is concentrated in the hands of very few major shareholders (La Porta et al., 1999; Claessens et al., 2000). Concentrated ownership enables controlling shareholders to extract private benefits at the expense of minority shareholders (Shleifer & Vishny, 1997).

In China, ownership structure is highly concentrated (Chen et al., 2009; Cheng et al., 2009; Firth et al., 2006a; Gul et al., 2010; Wang, 2005). For instance, Chen et al. (2009) present evidence that the median of the largest shareholder's holding was 42.61 percent at the end of 2004, but the median of the second largest shareholder's holding was just five percent, and the third merely 1.89 percent. Scholars have widely tested the effect of concentrated ownership structures on listed firms' performance and other corporate factors. For instance, Li et al. (2004) collect evidence on the tunneling of big shareholders, focusing on the embezzlement of funds and asset transfers related to mergers and acquisition; they find that concentrated ownership enhances asset appropriation by block-holding shareholders. Liu and Lu (2007) report a non-linear relationship between the largest shareholder's holdings and firms' earning management activities among Chinese listed firms. Lin, Ma, and Su. (2009) report a similar result of a U-shaped relationship between the shareholding of the largest shareholder and firm efficiency. Jiang et al. (2010) provide evidence of wealth tunneling in China by demonstrating the widespread practice of controlling shareholders of corporate loans to extract funds from firms. Berkman et al. (2009) show that publicly traded Chinese firms issued loan guarantees to their related parties (usually the controlling block holders), thereby expropriating wealth from minority shareholders. Lee and Xiao (2004), Lin et al. (2010), and Tang and Luo (2006) find that Chinese firms with concentrated ownership structures tend to pay higher cash dividends to meet the cash needs of the largest shareholders, which implies that large controlling shareholders are able to impose their preferred payout policy upon companies to reflect their own preference.

Additionally, the government retains substantial ownership of many listed firms to maintain its control or influence over state controlled enterprises (SOEs). Scholars have reported state ownership as an ineffective corporate governance mechanism in China. For instance, Sun and Tong (2003) find that share issue privatization - a reduction in state ownership - is associated with improved corporate performance. Bai et al. (2004) find that when the largest shareholder is the state, the firms tend to have lower market valuation. Li et al. (2004) find that companies controlled by the government or business groups experienced the most severe form of tunneling. Gunasekarage et al. (2007) find that, on average, firms' stock performance is negatively influenced by state ownership. However, such a negative relationship is significant only at high levels of government ownership. Conyon and He (2011) show that executive pay and CEO incentives are lower in state-controlled firms, and non-state (private) controlled firms are more likely to replace the CEO for poor performance.

Thirdly, managerial and employee shareholdings are extremely small in China's listed firms. At the end of 2004, management, foreign, and employee shares represented less than two percent of listed firms' outstanding shares, so these investors do not constitute major voting blocks (Chen et al. 2009). Managerial share ownership is typically less than one percent of the total shares on issue (Wei et al., 2005). Some studies have tested the significance of managerial shareholdings in China. Most of them report positive results. Gao and Kling (2008) report that managers' shareholdings are an effective governance mechanism for mitigating tunneling activities, although the economic significance is small. Li et al. (2007) examine the relationship between managerial ownership and firm performance for a sample of SOEs privatized over the period 1992—2000. Their results indicate that managerial ownership has a positive effect on firm performance. Based on Chinese non-listed firms, Hu and Zhou (2008) find that firms with significant managerial ownership levels outperform those whose managers do not own equity shares. In addition, Ning and Zhou (2005) find that employee stock ownership does not improve firm performance significantly in China, suggesting that negligible fractional ownership does not provide a meaningful employee incentive.

It has been widely documented that the non-tradability of shares was a main determinant of Chinese controlling shareholders' preferences for cash dividends, which conflicts with the interests of minority shareholder (Cheng et al., 2009; Huang et al., 2011; Wei & Xiao, 2009). For instance, Wei and Xiao (2009) find that tradable shareholders prefer stock dividends, and the non-tradable shareholders prefer cash dividends. Yi et al. (2007) study the dividend policy of Chinese listed companies during 2003 and 2004. They document that non-tradable shareholders prefer cash dividends rather than stock dividends, since the shares paid as dividends cannot be traded. On the other hand, stock dividends are preferred by tradable shareholders, as abnormal returns from stock dividends are significantly larger than those from cash dividends in the short-run.

2.2　Board of directors

It has been widely demonstrated through empirical studies that independent-director system is an effective corporate governance mechanism in developed countries (Dahya et al., 2008; Rosenstein & Wyatt, 1990; Weisbach, 1988). In China, the distinguishing characteristic of a board of directors is the mandatory high board independence.

However, literature on the effects of independent-director system in China is mixed. Kato and Long (2006a) report that independent directors strengthen the association between poor firm performance and CEO turnover. Fan et al. (2007) find that independent directors have a positive effect on CEO monitoring (CEO turnover). Gao and Kling (2008) analyze asset appropriation by principal shareholders in China and reveal that outsiders in the board of directors prevent operational tunneling. Conyon and He (2011) find that firms with more independent directors on the board have a higher pay-for-performance link, and firms with more independent directors on the board are more likely to replace the CEO for poor performance. In contrast, Chen et al. (2004) find that politicians and state controlling owners occupy most board seats, there are few professionals (lawyers, accountants, finance experts) on Chinese boards and almost no representation by minority shareholders. They argue that although the proportion of outsider directors on the board is high, the level of board independence and professionalism is not necessarily good. Further, based on 494 Chinese listed companies that began to recruit independent directors in 2002, Liao, Sun, and Young (2009) report that Chinese firms implement board independence by adding extra members instead of removing inside directors, except in the case where board size (before the recruitment of independent directors) was already too large. Using data on 1,117 Chinese listed firms that completed the share reform by the end of 2006, Qiu and Yao (2009) suggest that outside directors are not really independent and provide evidence that independent directors did not positively affect firm performance before or after the split-share reform. Consequently, it is crucial to ensure the independence of independent directors.

A second factor perceived to affect the board's ability to function effectively is the board's size. Lipton and Lorsch (1992) and Jensen (1993) suggest that larger boards could be less effective than smaller ones because of coordination problems and director free riding. Yermack (1996) and Eisenberg et al. (1998) provide evidence that smaller boards are associated with higher firm value, as measured by Tobin's Q. However, Coles et al (2008) argue that complex firms stand to benefit from having more directors on their boards, because CEOs of complex firms have a greater need for advice and expertise.

Researches on board size rarely find that size has a significant effect in China's listed firms. As an exception, Liao, Sun, and Young (2009) report that there exists a negative relationship between board size and firm performance. However, Tobin's Q increases in relation to board size for complex (large and diversified) firms.

2.3 CEO duality, CEO compensation, and CEO turnover

(1) CEO duality

The literature reports contradictory opinions about Chief Executive Officer (CEO) duality in developed countries. Some suggest that splitting the board chair and CEO provides more effective monitoring and control of the CEO; and firms that separate the two positions outperform those that do not (Rechner & Dalton, 1991). However, others argue that CEO duality establishes strong and unambiguous leadership and increases board efficiency. It is argued that firms with CEO duality can make better and faster decisions and hence outperform those without CEO duality [for example, Donaldson and Davis (1991)].

There is little research on CEO duality in China. Chen et al. (2009) find that the proportion of CEO duality in listed firms fell from 27.3 per cent to 13.8 per cent over the period 1999 to 2002; but they report that CEO duality has a statistically insignificant impact on firm efficiency. However, Bai et al. (2004) report a negative relationship between CEO duality and firm performance. Kato and Long (2006a) find that CEO duality reduces the probability of CEO turnover. Fan et al. (2007) find that CEO duality is marginally negatively related to CEO turnover.

(2) CEO compensation

A strong relation between compensation and firm performance would enable a better alignment of interests between shareholders and managers (Jensen & Murphy, 1990). Researchers have examined the relationship between compensation and firm performance, and find a positive relation between pay and performance (Barro & Barro, 1990; Jensen & Murphy, 1990; Kaplan, 1994; Rose & Shepard, 1994).

Existing literatures in China mainly investigate the linkage between CEO compensation and firm performance, and report mixed results. For instance, Firth et al. (2006a) report that firms that have private blockholders or SOEs as their major shareholders relate the CEO's pay to increases in stockholders' wealth or increases in profitability. However, the pay-performance sensitivities for CEOs are low and this raises questions about the effectiveness of firms' incentive systems. Firth et al. (2006a) argue that CEO compensation policy is used more as an instrument to achieve the dominant shareholders' objectives under the current concentrated ownership structure. Moreover, Firth et al. (2007) find no association between CEO's pay and firms' stock returns. In contrast, Kato and Long (2006b) investigate a sample of 937 publicly traded firms in China from 1998 to 2002. They find that executive cash compensation is positively related to firm performance. They also find some evidence that the pay-for-performance link is weaker in state-owned firms. Conyon and He (2011) use data on publically traded Chinese firms listed on domestic exchanges from 2001 to 2005, and find that executive compensation is positively correlated to firm performance.

(3) CEO turnover

The relationship between management turnover and poor firm performance is a good way of assessing the effectiveness of a firm's governance system and has been widely investigated in developed countries. Researchers have examined how well corporate governance mechanisms work, such as board composition, ownership structure, industry competition, and legal protection of investors, influence the effectiveness of CEO turnover (DeFond & Hung, 2004; DeFond & Park, 1999; Denis & Denis, 1995; Huson et al., 2004; Kang & Shivdasani, 1995; Weisbach, 1988).

In addition to studying the sensitivity of CEO turnover to firm performance, another approach in assessing CEO turnover quality is to investigate the subsequent firm performance. It is also documented that forced managerial turnover is followed by improved firm performance in developed countries (Huson et al., 2004; Kang & Shivdasani, 1995).

The evidence from China mainly investigates the sensitivity of turnover and performance, and how corporate governance mechanisms influence that sensitivity (Chi & Wang, 2009; Chang & Wong, 2009; Conyon & He, 2011; Firth et al., 2006b; Kato & Long, 2006a; Kato & Long, 2006b; Wang, 2010). For instance, Kato and Long (2006a) find evidence that CEO turnover is significantly and inversely related to firm performance, although the magnitude of the relationship is modest. In addition, they find that this turnover-performance link is weaker for listed firms that are still controlled by the state, and the appointment of independent directors enhances the turnover-performance link. Shen and Lin (2009) find that profitability and state ownership have a negative impact on top management turnover when profitability is below target (measured by industry median), but no impact when profitability is above target. Chang and Wong (2009) examine the relationship between CEO turnover and the performance of listed Chinese firms, and find a negative relationship between the level of pre-turnover profitability and CEO turnover when firms are incurring financial losses, but no such relationship when they are making profits. Conyon and He (2011) find that CEO turnover is negatively correlated to firm performance, and privately controlled firms and firms with more independent directors on the board are more likely to replace the CEO for poor performance.

Some studies have investigated firm performance following managerial turnover in China, and report improved performance. Kato and Long (2006b) examine CEO turnover of 634 listed firms from 1998 to 2002 and find that listed firms appear to subsequently experience greater improvement in performance (measured either as shareholder returns or return on assets) after the replacement of their CEOs when the firms are privately controlled or have a majority controlling shareholder. Shen and Lin (2009) find that top management turnover has a positive impact on subsequent firm profitability when it occurs under performance below target. Chang and Wong (2009) examine the post-turnover performance of China's listed firms and find that there is an improvement in post-turnover accounting performance in loss-making firms. However, these three studies focus exclusively on the pre-reform period (before split-share structure reform), and two of the three focus on performance measured by accounting performance.

2.4 External governance mechanisms

2.4.1 Takeover market

An active corporate control market is considered to be essential for the efficient allocation of resources (Bai et al., 2004). Companies with unsatisfactory performance are frequently disciplined by the market or takeovers when there is a dynamic takeover market.

Although an external corporate control market has been shown to be an effective governance mechanism in Western countries, this kind of market is not well developed in China. Chi et al. (2011) report that tender offers are still very rare and target firms are often not listed. They find a strong political connection between acquiring and target firms in most mergers and acquisitions (M&As) and a significantly positive impact on the acquiring firm's market performance. Due to the special characteristics of Chinese M&As caused by the share segmentation system, there is little literature about the effect of the hostile takeover market as an external corporate governance mechanism in China.

2.4.2 Product market competition

Previous studies have found that competition in product markets is an effective corporate governance mechanism (Alison & Mayes, 1991; Cuñat & Guadalupe, 2005; Hart, 1983; Haskel, 1991; Hay & Liu, 1997; Hermalin, 1994; Holmstrom, 1982; Nalebuff & Stiglitz, 1983). In China, SOE reforms were implemented in the 1990s, accompanied by the introduction of market competition. Market based competition tends to put greater pressure on firms' R&D to implement an efficient production process and produce competitive products (Liu & White, 2001). Some studies on the effectiveness of product market competition in China's firms have had positive results. For instance, firm-level studies show that an increase in the intensification of competition has significantly improved managerial incentives and total factor productivity of SOEs (Li, 1997). Using data on rural financial institutions in China, Park et al. (2003) empirically test the effects of competition on deposit growth, loan portfolio composition, repayment rates, and other effort measures, finding positive effects of competition on effort and financial performance.

2.4.3 Legal infrastructure

Bai et al. (2004) argue that legal infrastructure is an effective external mechanism to ensure investors receive a fair return on their investment. The Chinese stock market is less than 20 years old. It has been widely and severely criticized for its lack of a sound legal framework and effective law enforcement (Zou et al., 2008; Jiang et al., 2010). Jiang et al. (2010) point out that the legal system in China offers few options for minority shareholders to take private enforcement action against blockholders' misconduct. Furthermore, public enforcement, including fines and prison terms for tunneling, has been hampered by the limited authority of security market regulators.

2.4.4 Bank monitoring

Bank borrowing can enhance firm value by providing effective monitoring to borrowers. For instance, Ahn and Choi (2009) provide evidence that bank reputation, the size of loans, and the length of loan maturity reduce firms' earnings management activities in America. Byers et al. (2008) report an inverse relationship between loan announcement abnormal returns and internal governance variables and provide evidence that banks can be substitute monitors for internal governance mechanisms such as independent directors, CEO incentive-based pay, and director shareholdings.

In China, the four big state-owned banks still dominate the market (Berger et al., 2009). Some studies explore the role of banks as a corporate governance mechanism in China. For instance, Tian and Estrin (2007) have studied the impact of bank loans on firm performance. They argue that government banks would not provide effective governance to borrowers as the state usually sacrifices financial interests to social and political interests. The soft budget constraint is the key obstacle preventing banks from providing significant monitoring to firms since the state is still the ultimate owner of the major banks and most listed firms.[①] Lin, Zhang, and Zhu (2009) investigate the effect of bank ownership on firm value in China. They find that banks appoint board members through equity holdings, and companies with banks as leading shareholders witness relatively poor

---

① The soft budget constraint is a term coined by Kornai (1979) to describe state refinancing of unprofitable enterprises in socialist economies.

operating performance. Further analysis indicates that inefficient investments resulting from bank ownership are responsible for disappointing performance.

2.5 Summary of the literature review and research questions

This chapter has reviewed studies on corporate governance in China, and suggested that ① controlling shareholders expropriate minority shareholders' wealth in various ways; ② state ownership is an ineffective corporate governance mechanism; ③ evidences on the effects of independent directors, and the linkage between CEO compensation and firm performance is mixed; ④ top managers are likely to be replaced when firms' performance is poor; ⑤ the performance of underperforming firms improves following top management turnover; ⑥ effective external governance devices are almost absent in China.

Based on a review of the existing literature, this chapter also proposes specific research questions for this study: ① What was the relationship between corporate governance structure and firm performance during the financial crisis? ② Does firm stock performance following top management turnover improve? What has been the effect of split-share structure reform on stock performance improvement subsequent to managerial turnover? ③ How does the split-share structure reform influence the controlling shareholder's preference for cash dividends in China?

The relation between corporate governance and firm performance is a topic that has been most intensively analyzed in corporate governance research. Although there are existing works for China, it will be important to re-examine the issue in a research setting that is less subject to the endogeneity problem. Bai et al. (2009) and Lin, Zhang, and Zhu (2009) address this issue by using the firm-fixed effects model and two-stage least squares method. Meanwhile, previous studies suggest that usage of financial crisis data mitigates the endogeneity problem, because financial crisis is an unpredictable shock. I adopt this approach to analyze the relation between corporate governance and firm performance in this study. In addition, crisis-period data allow me to uncover some aspects of corporate governance mechanisms that are less pronounced during normal economic conditions (question ①; Chapter 3).

As mentioned previously, CEO turnover is a topic that has held the attention of many corporate governance researchers. However, previous studies lack analyses of CEO turnover during the post split-share structure reform period. The split-share reform potentially changes the incentive of controlling shareholders to discipline the CEO based on stock performance. Once a firm completes the reform, controlling shareholders are likely to have an incentive to replace management to increase stock prices (achieve capital gains). This idea motivates this study to address the second question in Chapter 4.

The split-share structure reform also provides me with a rich research opportunity on Chinese controlling shareholders' preference for cash dividends. Previous studies suggest that share non-tradability makes controlling shareholders prefer dividends. After the split-share structure reform, shares held by controlling shareholders become tradable, thus their preference for cash dividends should weaken, and consequently cash dividend levels are likely to decline. However, to the best of our knowledge, little academic attention has been paid to the impact of split-share structure reform on Chinese corporate cash dividend policy (question ③; Chapter 5).

3. Corporate governance and firm value during the global financial crisis: Evidence from China

3.1 Introduction

Numerous studies have investigated the relation between corporate governance structure and firm performance (Bhagat & Bolton, 2008; Dahya et al., 2008; Gompers et al., 2003; Klapper & Love, 2004; McConnell & Servaes, 1990, 1995; Morck et al., 1988). The present study addresses this issue for Chinese companies. China is of particular interest to corporate governance researchers because Chinese companies experience special agency problems. Shleifer and Vishny (1997) suggest that controlling shareholders is led by the incentive to pursue private benefits at the expense of minority shareholders.① In China, there are many state-owned enterprises

---

① La Porta et al. (1999) and Dharwadkar et al. (2000) argue that the greatest source of agency problems stem from controlling shareholders, who expropriate value from minority shareholders. Bebchuk et al. (2000) and Morck et al. (2000) discuss how controlling shareholders may pursue objectives that are at odds with those of minority shareholders. Morck et al. (2005) suggest that concentrated ownership, combined with an absence of effective external governance mechanisms, results in more frequent conflicts between controlling and minority shareholders.

(SOEs) in which a controlling shareholder (states) retains a strong power and pursue various public objectives (two-thirds of Chinese listed companies were SOEs at the end of 2006). Several researchers show evidence that SOEs exhibit poor performance (Bai et al., 2000; Sun & Tong, 2003; Zhang et al., 2001). In addition, Wei (2005) describes insider stock ownership in China as very small, suggesting that Chinese companies potentially improve performance by increasing managerial ownership. Indeed, Li et al. (2007) and Hu and Zhou (2008) offer evidence that firms perform better when their managers take equity stakes.

A problem that commonly plagues many corporate governance studies is endogeneity of corporate governance structures. In general, firms adopt governance structures to maximize their firm value in response to exogenous contracting environments. In this situation, exogenous factors determine both observed corporate governance structures and firm performance; as a result, it is difficult to accurately evaluate the effect of corporate governance on firm performance. An effective way to measure the effects of corporate governance on firm performance is to analyze stock price return during a financial crisis. A financial crisis is a sudden, unpredictable event; it is extremely difficult for firms to adjust their optimal corporate governance structures in response to a future financial crisis. In this situation, we can treat corporate governance structures as exogenous variables that explain firm performance during a subsequent financial crisis. Indeed, previous studies have investigated how corporate governance structures affected stock performance in emerging markets during the East Asian financial crisis of 1997—1998 (Baek et al., 2004; Johnson et al., 2000; Mitton, 2002; Lemmon & Lins, 2003). I also stress that stock returns during a crisis period serve as an appropriate measure of expropriation problems that are evident in countries with weak legal protection of investor rights (e.g., China). Insiders might distribute sufficient cash flow to outside investors as long as they have promising future prospects and seek further external financing (Johnson et al., 2000). Investors also tend to ignore a lack of adequate corporate governance structures during an economic boom (Rajan & Zingales, 1998). However, once a crisis begins and expected returns fall substantially, investors begin to consider corporate governance weaknesses, especially in countries where minority shareholder rights are not well protected (Mitton, 2002). Concerns about expropriation problems will lead to stock price declines; stock price performance during a crisis is likely to incorporate the expropriation of minority shareholders. To the best of my knowledge, few studies investigate how corporate governance affects firm performance in China during a financial crisis. This chapter intends to fill this research gap, re-examining how Chinese corporate governance structures affect firm performance in a research environment that is less subject to endogeneity problems. In addition, crisis-period data allow me to highlight some aspects of corporate governance mechanisms that are less pronounced during normal economic conditions. Kuppuswamy and Villalonga (2010) show evidence that US firms' diversification discounts become significantly small during the global financial crisis because internal capital markets mitigate financial constraints during the period. This story potentially holds true for Chinese SOEs that have preferential access to bank loans.

It is important to note that the analyses presented have important policy implications. In 2002, the CSRC issued Standards on Corporate Governance for Publicly Listed Companies, modeled on best corporate governance practices in the UK and US. The new 「Standards」 lay down a series of requirements for controlling shareholder behaviors as well as board composition and responsibilities, transparency, and information disclosure, etc. Since 2001, the CSRC and the two stock exchanges (Shanghai and Shenzhen) have issued similar regulations as to the content and quality of the annual financial reports and other disclosures released by listed companies (Lin, 2005). Our investigation examines whether such regulatory movements contribute to decreased expropriations of minority shareholders.

Using a comprehensive corporate governance data set of 970 Chinese firms, this chapter finds that SOEs that show significantly poor performance during a pre-crisis period experience small reductions in firm value during the crisis period. This chapter argues that state ownership mitigates the financial constraints that become severe during a financial crisis (Ivashina & Scharfstein, 2010; Kuppuswamy & Villalonga, 2010). Indeed, SOEs that rely more on bank debt experience fewer declines in firm value during the crisis period. In addition, the chapter finds that the crisis-period performance increases with large shareholders' ownership at high levels, although it decreases at low ownership levels (U-shaped relation). This result suggests that state ownership mitigates financial constraints and engenders expropriation problems. Previous studies stress that state ownership engenders expropriations of minority shareholders in normal economic conditions because the state pursues public objectives and induces overinvestment problems (Bai et al., 2000; Dewenter & Malatesta, 2001; Khwaja & Mian, 2005). In contrast, this chapter offers new evidence that state ownership stabilizes shareholder value during crisis periods. When firms face severe financial constraints, preferential access to bank debt attributable to state ownership brings high value to companies that exceeds the value-decreasing effect of state ownership.

This chapter also finds that high managerial ownership is positively associated with a change in firm value of SOEs during the crisis period after controlling for various firm characteristics. Consistent with Li et al.'s (2007) finding, this result supports the view that in Chinese SOEs that have public objectives, managerial ownership is an effective way of aligning managerial interests with those of minority shareholders. Finally, the chapter finds that firms that adopt a reputable accounting auditor experience small firm value reductions during the crisis. The result supports the idea that greater disclosure lessens information asymmetry and thereby mitigates agency conflicts between managers and outside investors (Diamond & Verrecchia, 1991; Glosten & Milgrom, 1985; Healy & Palepu, 2001; Meek et al., 1995). Together with the managerial ownership result, this finding presents additional evidence that strict corporate governance structures mitigate expropriation of minority shareholders, which becomes more severe during crisis periods (Baek et al., 2004; Lemmon & Lins, 2003; Mitton, 2002). The result also suggests that recent Chinese regulatory movements are steps in the right direction toward more effective corporate governance structures.

The chapter proceeds as follows. Section 2 presents hypotheses, while Section 3 describes the sample selection procedure and data. In Section 4, I present results of empirical analyses. Section 5 reports additional test results, while Section 6 summarizes and concludes the chapter.

3.2 Hypotheses

A distinctive feature of Chinese corporate governance is the existence of state control. Many previous Chinese studies have found a negative effect of state ownership on firm value (Gunasekarage et al., 2007; Sun & Tong, 2003; Xu & Wang, 1999; Zhang et al., 2001). It is likely that, in normal economic conditions, the expropriation of minority shareholders by the state exists. Shleifer and Vishny (1994) suggest that direct state ownership is associated with the pursuit of political objectives at the expense of other stakeholders in the firm. Bai et al. (2000) and Clarke (2003) argue that SOEs principally aim to maintain employment and social stability (public objectives) rather than profit maximization, which engenders agency conflicts between the state and minority shareholders. In addition, while state ownership enhances a firm's access to debt, it also has adverse effects on managerial incentives and firm performance (Dewenter & Malatesta, 2001; Khwaja & Mian, 2005). Chinese state-owned banks impose fewer restrictions on the capital budgeting decisions of poorly performing SOEs, and provide bailout loans to distressed SOEs; as a result, SOEs are likely to conduct value-decreasing investments (Firth et al., 2008). These facts give rise to the prediction that SOEs will suffer more from decreased firm value during a global financial crisis.

Regarding the effect of state ownership on firm value during a financial crisis, we can also make an opposite prediction. During financial crisis periods, companies tend to suffer from severe financial constraints (Ivashina & Scharfstein, 2010). Campello et al. (2010) find that during the credit crisis of 2008 financial constraints forced numerous firms to forgo attractive investment projects, particularly in Europe and Asia. Previous studies show that state-owned banks make decisions to provide loans in consideration of political interests (Din, 2005; Sapienza, 2004). As a result, Chinese SOEs receive a disproportionately large share of the credits provided by large state banks (Allen et al., 2005; Gordon & Li, 2003). Li, Yue, and Zhao (2009) show that Chinese SOEs receive preferential treatment and have easy access to bank funding. This characteristic potentially engenders overinvestment problems in typical economic conditions, but mitigates the severe financing constraints that plague numerous companies during financial crisis periods. Lu et al. (2005) suggest that the government tends to act as an implicit debt guarantor for firms with high state ownership. In addition, Deng and Wang (2006) argue that the government often rescues financially distressed firms. Those facts suggest outside investors are likely to believe SOEs suffer less from financial constraints and liquidity shortage during a financial crisis. Overall, state ownership potentially has both positive and negative effects on firm performance during a financial crisis. I propose two conflicting hypotheses because it is an open empirical question which effect prevails during a crisis period.

H1-1: *SOEs suffer more from reductions in firm value than non-SOEs during a global financial crisis.*

H1-2: *SOEs suffer less from reductions in firm value than non-SOEs during a global financial crisis.*

To explore the effect of state ownership, I construct a dummy variable (D_SOE) that equals one if government is the controlling shareholder and zero otherwise. I also adopt the proportion of shares owned by large shareholders (shareholders who own at least 5% of the firm's outstanding shares) (*LSOWN*) as a proxy for ownership concentration. Controlling shareholders (e.g., states) may exert power to benefit themselves at the expense of minority shareholders (Shleifer & Vishny, 1997). Indeed, Baek et al. (2004) provide evidence that Korean chaebol firms with concentrated ownership experienced a large drop in the value of their equity during the East Asian crisis. This is especially true for Chinese companies in which the government retains strong power. H1-1 predicts that *LSOWN* has a negative impact on firm performance during a financial crisis. In contrast, *LSOWN* will have a positive impact on performance during a crisis period if firms with high state ownership can more easily access bank loans (H1-2). We also use bank debt divided by assets (*BANKR*) as a measure of a firm's reliance on bank loans from state-owned banks. Given that the state provides credits via state-owned bank lending to SOEs, *BANKR* will have a positive impact on firm value during times of financial crisis (H1-2).

My first hypothesis (H1-1) assumes that severe expropriation problems exist in SOEs. This problem is potentially mitigated by managerial ownership. Previous US studies have found evidence that firm value increases with managerial ownership at certain ownership levels (McConnell & Servaes, 1990, 1995; Morck et al., 1988). Several papers investigate the relationship between firm performance and managerial ownership for Chinese companies. Differently from the US case where low managerial ownership engenders agency conflicts between shareholders and managers, managerial ownership potentially mitigates expropriation problems in China that are attributable to concentrated ownership structure (or high state ownership). Li et al. (2007) find a monotonically positive relationship between managerial ownership and performance changes for Chinese SOEs. These discussions give rise to the following hypothesis.

H2: *Firms with high managerial ownership suffer less from deteriorating firm value during a global financial crisis.*

In this chapter, percentage ownership by the CEO and executive directors (hereafter denoted by *MOWN*) is used as a proxy for managerial ownership (see Table 3.1 for definitions of variables). Previous US studies find a negative relation between firm value and managerial ownership at certain ownership levels (McConnell & Servaes, 1990, 1995; Morck et al., 1988). However, the average managerial ownership in Chinese companies is so low that entrenchment effects are unlikely. For this reason, this chapter predicts a monotonically positive relation between firm performance and managerial ownership.

Table 3.1   Definitions of variables

Variables	Definition
Ch_Q	Change in Tobin's Q from August 2007 through December 2008. Tobin's Q is defined as the ratio of total liabilities and market value of equity divided by the book value of total assets.
D_SOE	Dummy variable that takes the value of one for firms in which the controlling shareholder is the government.
BANKR	Bank debt divided by total assets.
LSOWN	Percentage ownership by the large shareholders. We define large shareholders as owners who hold at least 5% of the firm's outstanding shares.
MOWN	Percentage ownership by the CEO and executive directors.
BOARDSIZE	Natural logarithm of the number of directors.
INDBOARD	Number of independent directors divided by the number of total board members.
DUALITY	Dummy variable that takes the value of one if the CEO also serves as the chairman or vice chairman of the board of directors.
BIG_FOUR	Dummy variable that takes the value of one for firms that adopt a Big Four accounting firm as the auditor and zero otherwise.
BSHARE	Dummy variable that takes a value of one for firms that issue B-shares and zero otherwise.
LEV	Total liabilities minus bank debt divided by total assets.
LIQUID	Ratio of current liabilities to current assets.

Table3. 1(continued)

Variables	Definition
EXPORTR	Export sales divided by total sales.
ROA	Earnings before interest and tax divided by total assets.
B_M	Book value of equity divided by the market value of equity.
STD	Standard deviation of monthly stock returns from August 2006 to July 2007.
LN_MVALUE	Natural logarithm of market value of equity.

3.3 Sample selection and data

The sample comprises Chinese firms listed on the Shanghai and Shenzhen Stock Exchanges. The chapter collects financial and stock price data from the Osiris database. Then, I merge corporate governance data obtained from the CCER database with the financial and stock price data. The chapter deletes financial institutions (firms that have a CSRC industrial classification code that begins with 「I」) from the analyses because their financial statement formats are different from those of non-financial firms.

Following Ivashina and Scharfstein (2010), the chapter defines the financial crisis period as August 2007 through December 2008. The chapter uses the change in Tobin's Q during the period (Ch_Q) as a proxy for change in firm value during the financial crisis; Tobin's Q is computed as the ratio of total liabilities and the market value of equity divided by the book value of total assets. Key independent variables are D_SOE, $BANKR$, $LSOWN$, and $MOWN$.

The analyses include several control variables that potentially affect firm value during the financial crisis. The board of directors is an instrument through which shareholders can exert influence on the behavior of managers to ensure the company is run according to their interests (Hermalin & Weisbach, 2003). Fama (1980) argues that boards of directors are the central internal control mechanisms for monitoring managers. Since the Sarbanes Oxley (Sox) Act mandates that the audit committees for the boards of directors of listed companies have a majority of independent members, corporate board structures have received much attention from researchers lately (Boone et al., 2007; Coles et al., 2008; Guest, 2008;). This chapter focuses on two aspects of board structures: board size and independence. The literature shows that large boards are less effective than smaller boards due to free-rider problems (Gladstein, 1984; Jensen, 1993; Lipton & Lorsch, 1992; Shaw, 1981). Bennedsen et al. (2008), Eisenberg et al. (1998), and Yermack (1996) offer evidence that small boards are accompanied by high firm value. In this chapter, a natural logarithm of the number of directors ($BOARDSIZE$) is used as a proxy for board size.

It is well documented that independent directors monitor management more in the interests of shareholders than inside directors do (Fama, 1980; Fama & Jensen, 1983a; Jensen, 1993). Some researchers present evidence that supports the effective monitoring role of independent boards. For example, using an event study methodology, Rosenstein and Wyatt (1990) find a significantly positive stock price reaction to the announcement of outsider appointments to boards. Examining 128 tender offer bids during the period 1980 through 1987, Byrd and Hickman (1992) show that bidding firms in which independent outside directors hold at least 50 percent of the seats have significantly higher announcement returns than other bidders. Using data from the UK, Dahya and McConnell (2005) conclude that boards with a greater proportion of outside directors make different (perhaps better) decisions. More recently, Dahya et al. (2008) find a positive relationship between board independence and operating performance. Calls for independent boards have become increasingly evident in China; the CSRC promulgated a regulation requiring listed companies to have independent directors account for at least one-third of the firm's total board members by June 30, 2003 (CSRC, 2001). This chapter adopts the proportion of independent directors over total board members (*INDBOARD*) as a proxy for board independence.[①]

In addition, previous studies suggest that a person serving both as board chairman and CEO can exert power to pursue his or her private benefits at the expense of shareholder wealth (Jensen, 1993). Several researchers argue that the same person should not occupy both seats because such a dual role reduces the effectiveness of board monitoring (Finkelstein & D'Aveni, 1994; Mallette & Fowler, 1992). In contrast, Dechow et al. (1996) and Peng et al. (2007) find a positive relationship between CEO duality and firm performance. This chapter adopts a dummy variable that equals one if the firm's CEO also serves as its board chairman or vice chairman and zero otherwise (*DUALITY*), to test the effect of CEO duality on firm value during the crisis.

Quality of information disclosure has received much attention from recent corporate governance literature. The idea that greater disclosure lowers information asymmetry and thereby mitigates agency conflicts between managers and outside investors is well cited (Bushman & Smith, 2001; Diamond & Verrecchia, 1991; Glosten & Milgrom, 1985; Healy & Palepu, 2001; Hope & Thomas, 2008; Meek et al., 1995). Indeed, Leuz et al. (2009) find that in countries with poor disclosure requirements, foreign investors invest less money in firms with high family control. Information disclosure quality becomes particularly important during crisis periods, when expropriations of minority shareholders are likely to occur. Mitton (2002) and Baek et al. (2004) find that better disclosure was associated with higher firm performance during the East Asian crisis. Following Mitton (2002), this chapter adopts a dummy variable that takes the value of one when the firm's auditor is one of the four largest international accounting firms in order to measure the firm's disclosure quality. The largest international ac-

---

[①] Liu et al. (2011) show evidence that Japanese firms that have more independent boards are less likely to decrease dividends and more likely to experience management turnover during a global financial crisis.

counting firms (the Big Four) are: Pricewaterhouse Coopers, Deloitte Touche Tohmatsu, Ernst & Young, and KPMG. The Big Four auditors are likely to improve the quality of information disclosure for the following reasons: ① Big Four firms have a greater reputation to uphold (Michaely and Shaw, 1995); ② they are more independent than local firms; ③ they are exposed to greater legal liabilities for errors (Dye, 1993). In addition, Big Four auditors may allay investor fears during financial crises due to their prominent reputations (Rahman, 1998).

Companies that issue B-shares, which are traded mainly by foreign investors in foreign currencies, must adopt international accounting standards. Hence, B-share issuance serves as a proxy for better corporate governance. Baek et al. (2004) show that Korean firms that were owned more by unaffiliated foreign shareholders experienced smaller stock price reductions during the East Asian crisis. Bai et al. (2004) find that B-share issuance to foreigners has a positive effect on market valuation. Thus, this chapter adopts a dummy variable that equals one if a company issues B-shares traded on the Shanghai Stock Exchange or the Shenzhen Stock Exchange and zero otherwise (hereafter denoted by *BSHARE*).

Firms with high leverage inevitably experience poor stock price performance during economic downturns (Lang & Stulz, 1992; Opler & Titman, 1994). Total liabilities minus bank debt divided by total assets (*LEV*) is used to control for the leverage effect. Given that previous studies show evidence that corporate investment levels are positively related to liquidity (Fazzari et al., 1988; Hoshi et al., 1991; Whited, 1992), firms with poor liquidity conditions are forced to develop more investment plans, especially during a financial crisis. This chapter predicts that firms with greater liquidity experience smaller reductions in stock prices. This chapter adopts the ratio of current liabilities to current assets (*LIQUID*) as a measure of a firm's liquidity status.

It is likely that severe reductions in US consumption have unfavorable impacts on Chinese exporters. This chapter includes export sales divided by total sales (*EXPORTR*) to test this view; export sales data is obtained from firms' annual reports. In addition, this chapter includes return on assets (earnings before interests and taxes divided by total assets; *ROA*), book-to-market ratio (book value of equity divided by market value of equity; *B_M*), stock volatility (standard deviation of monthly stock returns from August 2006 to July 2007; *STD*), firm size (natural logarithm of the market value of equity; *LNMVALUE*), and industry dummies in all regressions. This chapter computes all variables except *STD* using year 2006 data in order to mitigate endogeneity problems. When necessary data is not available, this chapter deletes the firm from the analysis. In addition, this chapter deletes observations with *Ch_Q* greater (lower) than the 99th (1st) percentile to avoid outlier effects. As a result, the final sample includes 970 firms.

Table 3.2 reports descriptive statistics for the entire sample. Panel A presents summary statistics for the dummy variables. The government controls approximately 67% of the sample companies (SOEs). Only 6.6% of the sample firms employ one of the Big Four accounting firms as their auditor. Panel B summarizes descriptive statistics for the non-dummy variables. The mean and median declines in Tobin's Q are −2.1 and −1.5, respectively, which indicates that Chinese companies lose a substantial portion of their value during a global crisis period. The mean *MOWN* is about 1%, which indicates that there is great separation between ownership and management in Chinese companies (Wei, 2005). It is noteworthy that low managerial ownership is especially evident in SOEs; the mean *MOWN* is 0.13% for SOEs, which is significantly lower than that of non-SOEs (3.32%). Nevertheless, the sample firms have concentrated ownership structures, at least partly because the state holds substantial equity stakes in SOEs; the mean *LSOWN* is 46.3%. Independent directors account for about one third of total board members.

Table 3.2   **Descriptive statistics**

Panel A of this table shows descriptive statistics for the non-dummy variables, while Panel B presents the number (%) of firms that take a value of one for the dummy variables. The sample comprises 970 Chinese firms listed on the Shanghai Securities Exchange and the Shenzhen Stock Exchange.

Panel A: Dummy Variables ($N=970$)

Variable	Number of observations that take a value of one	%
BIG_FOUR	64	6.60%
D_SOE	649	66.91%
DUALITY	99	10.21%
BSHARE	69	7.11%

Panel B: Non-Dummy Variables ($N=970$)

Variable	Mean	STD	Min	P50	Max
Ch_Q	-2.133	2.084	-15.891	-1.535	0.382
BANKR	0.061	0.094	0.000	0.019	0.604
MOWN	0.012	0.064	0.000	0.000	0.690
LSOWN	0.463	0.157	0.052	0.468	0.943
BOARDSIZE	2.221	0.225	1.386	2.197	2.996
INDBOARD	0.355	0.051	0.125	0.333	0.75
LEV	0.520	0.345	0.021	0.505	7.537
LIQUID	1.140	1.240	0.018	0.889	22.467
EXPORTR	0.104	0.202	0.000	0.000	0.994
ROA	0.041	0.083	-1.379	0.043	0.297
B_M	1.243	3.947	-5.801	0.540	73.310
STD	0.203	0.135	0.000	0.191	2.961
LN_MVALUE	14.278	1.184	9.433	14.227	18.837

3.4 Empirical analyses

3.4.1 Univariate analyses

To test hypotheses, I divide the sample firms into several groups by D_SOE, $MOWN$, $LSOWN$, and $BANKR$ and compare Ch_Q across groups (see Table 3.3). For D_SOE, I simply divide the sample firms into two

Table 3.3   Univariate test results

This table compares changes in Tobin's Q (Ch_Q) for the subsamples. The sample comprises 970 Chinese firms listed on the Shanghai and Shenzhen Stock Exchanges. I divide the sample into several groups based on a corporate governance variable. For D_SOE I divide the entire sample into two groups (Group 1 is SOEs and Group 2 is non-SOEs). For $LSOWN$, I divide the sample equally into four groups. For $MOWN$ and $BANKR$, which take a value of zero for many observations, I make a group that consists of zero observations and divide the remaining firms equally into three groups. Presented figures are the mean Ch_Q (above) and the number of observations (in parentheses). The right-most column reports p-values for the null hypothesis: that the mean of Ch_Q is identical for the highest and lowest groups. See Table 3.1 for definitions of variables.

	Group	1 (Highest)	2	3	4 (Lowest)	p-value
D_SOE	Mean (N)	-2.032 (649)			-2.338 (321)	0.032
LSOWN	Mean (N)	-2.199 (242)	-2.387 (243)	-2.052 (243)	-1.886 (243)	0.095
BANKR	Mean (N)	-1.704 (207)	-2.045 (206)	-1.894 (207)	-2.581 (350)	0.000
MOWN	Mean (N)	-2.145 (216)	-2.058 (215)	-2.012 (216)	-2.257 (323)	0.556
MOWN (SOEs)	Mean (N)	-1.964 (147)	-2.069 (147)	-1.713 (148)	-2.283 (207)	0.173
MOWN (Non-SOEs)	Mean (N)	-2.480 (68)	-1.971 (68)	-2.774 (69)	-2.209 (116)	0.255

groups (Group 1 comprises firms for which the dummy variable takes the value of one). For *LSOWN*, I divide the sample equally into four groups. *MOWN* and *BANKR* take the value of zero for many firms; I make a group (Group 4) that comprises all firms for which a variable takes the value of zero; then, I divide the remaining firms equally into three groups (Group 1 is the highest group).

Table 3.3 shows that SOEs suffer less from firm value reductions than non-SOEs do. In addition, Table 3.3 shows that the highest *BANKR* group (Group 1) experiences significantly smaller declines in firm value than the lowest *BANKR* group (Group 4). Those results are consistent with the positive effect hypothesis (H1-2). The crisis-period performance decreases with *LSOWN* at low ownership levels; this result is consistent with H1-1, suggesting that ownership concentration engenders expropriation problems during a crisis. However, the highest *LSOWN* group (Group 1) has better performance than Group 2. It is likely that the large shareholders' ownership has a nonlinear relation to Ch_Q. Table 3.3 does not offer evidence that managerial ownership is significantly related to a decline in firm value during the global financial crisis. Li et al. (2007) find a monotonically positive relationship between managerial ownership and performance changes for SOEs. That is why we separately divide SOEs and non-SOEs into four groups by managerial ownership and compare the crisis-period performance. Neither SOEs nor non-SOEs present a monotonic positive relation between managerial ownership and Ch_Q.

3.4.2 Regression results

In this section, I present the regression results to investigate whether the corporate governance variables affect Ch_Q after controlling for various factors. To examine potential multicollinearity problems, I present a correlation matrix (see Table 3.4). The key independent variables (*D_SOE*; *LSOWN*; *BANKR*; *LSOWN*) have no serious, high correlations with other independent variables.

Table 3.4

Correlation matrix

	Ch_Q	D_SOE	BANKR	LSOWN	MOWN	BOARDSIZE	INDBOARD	DUALITY	BIG_FOUR	BSHARE	LEV	LIQUID	EXPORTR	ROA	B_M	STD	LN[M]
Ch_Q	1.00																
D_SOE	0.07	1.00															
BANKR	0.13	0.11	1.00														
LSOWN	-0.03	0.13	0.03	1.00													
MOWN	-0.05	-0.23	-0.08	-0.01	1.00												
BOARDSIZE	0.08	0.17	0.15	0.07	-0.06	1.00											
INDBOARD	-0.02	-0.08	-0.03	-0.02	0.06	-0.29	1.00										
DUALITY	-0.05	0.01	0.02	-0.04	0.02	-0.00	0.00	1.00									
BIG_FOUR	0.11	0.10	0.14	0.26	-0.03	0.16	0.02	-0.02	1.00								
BSHARE	0.21	0.06	-0.03	-0.04	-0.05	0.01	0.04	0.01	0.15	1.00							
LEV	0.10	-0.06	-0.14	-0.06	-0.06	0.01	-0.02	-0.04	-0.06	-011	1.00						
LIQUID	0.05	0.05	0.09	0.03	-0.07	0.06	-0.02	-0.05	0.08	0.08	0.59	1.00					
EXPORTR	0.03	-0.01	-0.10	0.02	0.11	-0.00	0.02	-0.04	0.04	0.10	-0.01	-0.09	1.00				
ROA	-0.13	0.04	0.03	0.08	0.09	0.07	0.02	0.04	0.09	-0.06	-0.27	-0.12	0.00	1.00			
B_M	0.19	0.04	0.03	0.00	-0.04	0.02	-0.00	0.04	0.14	0.55	-0.05	-0.04	0.09	-0.02	1.00		
STD	-0.01	-0.06	0.06	-0.07	-0.04	-0.11	0.01	-0.03	-0.13	-0.04	0.03	0.01	-0.04	-0.12	-0.01	1.00	
LN_MVALUE	-0.28	0.16	0.12	0.19	-0.01	0.16	-0.02	0.03	0.23	-0.47	-0.20	-0.07	-0.05	0.30	-0.38	-0.15	1.00

Regression results are presented in Table 3.5. As with the univariate test result, Models 1 to 3 show that the coefficient on D_SOE is positive and statistically significant at the 0.05 level. This result indicates that state ownership has a favorable impact on firm value during the crisis period. Consistent with this idea, the coefficient on $BANKR$ is positive and significant at the 0.01 level. This chapter interprets this to mean that SOEs receive preferential access to bank debt, and as a result, avoid forgoing prospective projects (Li, Yue & Zhao, 2009). To further test this idea, Model 3 includes the interaction term D_SOE with $BANKR$; the interaction term has a positive and significant coefficient, as do D_SOE and $BANKR$. Consistent with the positive effect hypothesis, SOEs that rely on bank debt experience small reductions in Tobin's Q.

The models allow $LSOWN$ to have a non-linear relation to Ch_Q. As with the univariate test result, Table 3.5 shows evidence that the large shareholders' ownership has a U-shaped relation to the crisis-period firm performance; the estimated coefficients suggest that performance increases when large shareholders' ownership exceeds 57%. This result is attributable to the fact that SOEs tend to have high $LSOWN$. In unreported analyses, I adopt the interaction term between D_SOE and $LSOWN$ instead of the squared term of $LSOWN$. This regression analysis engenders a negative and significant coefficient on $LSOWN$, which suggests that ownership concentration engenders expropriation problems for non-SOEs. However, the interaction term of D_SOE and $LSOWN$ has a positive and statistically significant coefficient (at the 0.01 level), suggesting that SOEs with concentrated ownership structures experienced less declines in firm value. This result is consistent with the underlying idea of H1－2 that state ownership brings preferential access to bank debt and thereby mitigates financial constraints and liquidity shortage during a crisis period.

Table 3.5 Regression results for the crisis period:
August 2007 to December 2008

The table reports regression results of the change in Tobin's Q during the global financial crisis: August 2007 to December 2008. The sample comprises 970 Chinese firms listed on the Shanghai and Shenzhen Stock Exchanges. Year 2006 data are used for all independent variables except for STD, which is computed using monthly stock price data over the August 2006 to July 2007 period. Model 4 adopts only SOEs for investigation. Figures in parentheses are t-statistics. See Table 3.1 for definitions of variables.

	Model 1	Model 2	Model 3	Model 4
D_SOE	0.30** (2.02)	0.32** (2.12)	0.30** (2.00)	
BANKR	3.28*** (5.21)	3.28*** (5.21)	2.84*** (4.43)	3.27*** (4.52)
SOE * BANKR			5.2E−07** (3.74)	
LSOWN	−8.54*** (−4.71)	−8.51*** (−4.67)	−7.76*** (−4.20)	−7.82*** (−3.64)
$LSOWN^2$	7.50*** (4.32)	7.48*** (4.30)	6.65*** (3.73)	7.69*** (3.97)
MOWN	−0.51 (−0.47)	2.96 (0.77)	−0.56 (−0.51)	12.47*** (4.19)
$MOWN^2$		−7.45 (−0.92)		
BOARDSIZE	0.66* (1.84)	0.67* (1.90)	0.64* (1.79)	0.70 (1.49)
INDBOARD	0.15 (0.12)	0.19 (0.15)	0.22 (0.17)	0.94 (0.61)
DUALITY	−0.20 (−0.86)	−0.21 (−0.88)	−0.20 (−0.85)	−0.22 (−0.65)
BIG_FOUR	1.06*** (3.89)	1.05*** (3.85)	0.88*** (3.20)	0.93*** (2.91)
BSHARE	0.19 (0.73)	0.20 (0.79)	0.18 (0.70)	0.26 (0.86)
LEV	0.67** (2.14)	0.68** (2.16)	0.66** (2.11)	0.52 (1.29)

Table3.5(continued)

LIQUID	−0.15** (−2.25)	−0.15** (−2.26)	−0.16** (−2.29)	−0.11* (−1.83)
EXPORTR	0.17 (0.46)	0.15 (0.40)	0.14 (0.37)	0.29 (0.85)
ROA	−0.90 (−0.61)	−0.94 (−0.64)	−0.82 (−0.57)	−1.71 (−0.59)
B_M	0.02 (0.89)	0.02 (0.92)	0.01 (0.86)	0.03** (2.08)
STD	−0.78 (−1.33)	−0.76 (−1.31)	−0.73 (−1.24)	−0.71 (−0.93)
LN_MVALUE	−0.55*** (−5.99)	−0.55*** (−5.95)	−0.58*** (−6.12)	−0.49*** (−4.17)
INDUSTRY	Yes	Yes	Yes	Yes
N	970	970	970	649
Adjusted R^2	0.20	0.20	0.21	0.23

*** : Significant at the 1% level; ** : Significant at the 5% level; * : Significant at the 10% level.

This chapter also conducts additional analyses that categorize sample companies into four groups: SOEs with bank debt, non-SOEs with bank debt, SOEs without bank debt, and non-SOEs without bank debt. This chapter uses dummy variables indicating the firm's category and find that SOEs with bank debt and non-SOEs with bank debt have significantly better performance during the financial crisis than non-SOEs without bank debt (results not reported). The estimated coefficients suggest that SOEs with bank debt outperform non-SOEs with bank debt which suggests that SOEs with bank loans experienced the lowest declines in firm value during the financial crisis due to preferential access to bank debt. I tried to collect information on the proportion of bank loan borrowed by SOEs, and provide news though not during our sample period that indicates government investment as well as bank loans typically went to SOEs (see Appendix 1).

The positive bank debt effect is in sharp contrast to the popular view that firms that rely on bank debt have few alternative financing sources and thus suffer more when banks decrease lending (Baek et al., 2004; Kang & Stultz, 2000; Nogata et al., 2010). This chapter interprets this evidence as parallel to empirical results on corporate diversification, as found by Kuppuswamy and Villalonga (2010).[①] Previous studies suggest that diversification has a negative impact on firm value (Berger & Ofek, 1995; Denis et al., 1997b; Lang & Stulz, 1994). However, Kuppuswamy and Villalonga (2010) show evidence that US firms' diversification discounts became significantly small during the global financial crisis. They argue that this decreased diversification discount is partly attributable to a 「more money effect」 that arises from the debt coinsurance feature of conglomerates.

Numerous studies show a non-linear relation between firm value and managerial ownership (McConell & Servaes, 1990, 1995; Morck et al., 1988; Short & Keasey, 1999). To address this issue, this chapter conducts regression analysis that includes the squared term of MOWN (Model 2). Models 1 and 2 indicate that, for the entire sample, managerial ownership had no significant impact on stock price performance during the financial crisis. Li et al. (2007) find a monotonically positive relationship between managerial ownership and performance changes for a sample of Chinese SOEs. This gives rise to a prediction that managerial ownership mitigates expropriation problems in SOEs that have powerful controlling shareholders. Model 4 replicates Model 1, using 649 SOE sample firms to test this idea. Although the univariate analysis does not find a positive relation between MOWN and Ch_Q, Model 4 engenders a positive and significant coefficient on MOWN. The result provides support for Li et al.'s (2007) findings in a research setting less subject to endogeneity problems.

With respect to other variables, all models engender a positive and

---

[①] Similarly, Nogata et al. (2010) show evidence that Japanese firms with more cross-held shareholders, which engender entrenchment effects in normal economic conditions, suffered less from deteriorating stock price performance during the financial crisis. This evidence, which is contrary to previous Japanese study findings, can also be viewed as parallel to our bank debt result.

significant coefficient on *BIG_FOUR*, which indicates that firms with better disclosure quality suffer less from stock price declines during a crisis period. Together with the *LSOWN* and *MOWN* results, this finding provides additional support for the view that corporate governance is an important determinant of firm value during a crisis period (Baek et al., 2004; Johnson et al., 2000; Mitton, 2002; Lemmon & Lins, 2003). Neither *BOARDSIZE* nor *INDBOARD* is associated with Ch_Q at the 0.05 significance level. Board characteristics have no explanatory power of variations in firm value change during the crisis. On the corporate boards of Chinese firms, there are a few professionals (lawyers, accountants, and finance experts) but there is almost no minority shareholder representation (Chen et al., 2004). As a result, board independence is highly compromised (Liu, 2006). Thus, it is likely such boards do not effectively monitor management. Table 3.5 suggests that *DUALITY* has an insignificant coefficient. Differently from US firms, Chinese companies are nearly under the control of the state; almost all senior executives are appointed by the controlling shareholder (Chen et al., 2006). This chapter interprets the result to mean that serving both as CEO and board chair does not give the individual dictatorship. Accordingly, as with the result on bank debt, *LEV* has a positive and significant coefficient. Consistent with the idea that firms with poor liquidity suffer more during crisis periods, *LIQUID* has a negative and significant coefficient. Table 3.5 also suggests that large firms suffer more during crisis periods. This chapter does not find a significant coefficient on *BSHARE*, *EXPORTR*, *ROA*, and *B_M*.

3.5 Additional tests

3.5.1 Differing definitions of financial crisis periods

In former analyses, this chapter defined the financial crisis period as August 2007 to December 2008. However, the Chinese stock price indices

(Shanghai Composite Index and Shenzhen Component Index) increased slightly from August 2007 to September 2007. Chinese stock prices began to decline significantly from October 2007, and the downward trend did not end until October 2008. Over the period, the Shanghai Composite Index and Shenzhen Component Index dropped by 70.96% and 70.10%, respectively.

This chapter adopts a new definition of the crisis period from October 2007 to October 2008 to test whether or not the results are sensitive to a definition of the global financial crisis. Table 3.6 presents qualitatively the same regression results for this period. Consistent with H1-2, *D_SOE*, *BANKR*, and *SOE * BANKR* have a positive and significant coefficient; Chinese SOEs faced fewer financing constraints and experienced less decline in firm value during the global financial crisis.① In addition, *LSOWN* has a U-shaped relation to the crisis-period performance, which suggests that high state ownership mitigates financial constraints and engenders expropriation problems.② *MOWN* has a positive and significant coefficient for the SOE subsample, suggesting that managerial ownership has a positive impact on the SOEs' crisis-period performance when I control for various firm characteristics. All models engender a positive and significant coefficient on *BIG_FOUR*, which suggests that better quality of information disclosure mitigates the expropriations of minority shareholders. Differently from the former regression, Table 3.6 engenders a positive and significant coefficient on *BOARDSIZE*. As with Coles et al. (2008), the result suggests that small boards, which certain previous studies view as more effective monitoring agents do not necessarily mitigate minority shareholder

---

① As with analyses for the period August 2007 to December 2008, unreported analyses show that SOEs with bank debt and non-SOEs with bank debt have significantly better performance during this period than non-SOEs without bank debt do. The estimated coefficients suggest that SOEs with bank debt outperform non-SOEs with bank debt.

② Again, unreported analyses that adopt the interaction term between *D_SOE* and *LSOWN* engender a negative and significant coefficient on *LSOWN* and a positive and significant coefficient on the interaction term.

wealth expropriations (Bennedsen et al., 2008; Eisenberg et al., 1998; Gladstein, 1984; Jensen, 1993; Lipton & Lorsch, 1992; Shaw, 1981; Yermack, 1996).

Table 3.6   Regression results for the crisis period: October 2007 to October 2008

	Model 1	Model 2	Model 3	Model 4
D_SOE	0.38** (2.42)	0.38** (2.41)	0.37** (2.40)	
BANKR	3.07*** (4.91)	3.07*** (4.91)	2.64*** (4.13)	2.96*** (4.12)
SOE * BANKR			5.2E-07** (3.13)	
LSOWN	-8.56*** (-5.08)	-8.55*** (-5.07)	-7.77*** (-4.49)	-7.87*** (-3.99)
$LSOWN^2$	7.50*** (4.56)	7.50*** (4.56)	6.66*** (3.89)	7.58*** (4.23)
MOWN	-0.16 (-0.19)	-0.18 (-0.05)	-0.21 (-0.24)	11.52*** (3.23)
$MOWN^2$		0.03 (-0.00)		
BOARDSIZE	0.71** (2.09)	0.71** (2.10)	0.69** (2.03)	0.81* (1.92)
INDBOARD	-0.37 (-0.25)	-0.37 (-0.25)	-0.30 (-0.20)	0.61 (0.32)
DUALITY	0.01 (0.05)	0.01 (0.05)	0.01 (0.06)	0.18 (0.65)
BIG_FOUR	0.93*** (3.46)	0.93*** (3.46)	0.74*** (2.77)	0.79** (2.52)

The table reports regression results of the change in Tobin's Q during the global financial crisis: October 2007 to October 2008. The sample comprises Chinese firms listed on the Shanghai Securities and Shenzhen Stock Exchanges. Year 2006 data are used for all independent variables except for STD, which is computed using monthly stock price data during the August 2006 to July 2007 period. Model 4 adopts only SOEs for investigation. Figures in parentheses are t-statistics. See Table 3.1 for definitions of variables.

Table3.6(continued)

BSHARE	0.08 (0.29)	0.08 (0.29)	0.07 (0.27)	0.21 (0.73)
LEV	0.50* (1.79)	0.50* (1.79)	0.48* (1.75)	0.38 (1.03)
LIQUID	-0.09 (-1.51)	-0.09 (-1.51)	-0.10 (-1.56)	-0.05 (-1.11)
EXPORTR	0.15 (0.40)	0.15 (0.41)	0.12 (0.32)	0.32 (1.03)
ROA	-0.45 (-0.32)	-0.45 (-0.32)	-0.37 (-0.27)	-1.35 (-0.48)
B_M	0.02 (1.07)	0.02 (1.07)	0.02 (1.05)	0.03** (2.13)
STD	-0.58 (-1.00)	-0.58 (-1.00)	-0.53 (-0.91)	-0.62 (-0.87)
LN_MVALUE	-0.52*** (-5.49)	-0.52*** (-5.50)	-0.54*** (-5.72)	-0.44*** (-3.87)
INDUSTRY	Yes	Yes	Yes	Yes
N	970	970	970	649
Adjusted R^2	0.17	0.17	0.18	0.20

*** : Significant at the 1% level; ** : Significant at the 5% level; * : Significant at the 10% level.

3.5.2 Deletion of outliers

Table 3.2 suggests that some sample firms have extremely low Ch_Q (the minimum is -15.9), although I delete observations with Ch_Q greater (lower) than the 99th (1st) percentile in the original sample. Table 3.2 also indicates that some sample firms have abnormally high B_M (the maximum is 73). To test if the main results are highly affected by these outliers, this chapter deletes firms that meet the following condition and conduct the same regression analysis: $Ch\_Q \leqslant -4.5$; $B\_M \geqslant 10$.

The regression analysis engenders qualitatively the same results (not reported): ① SOEs that rely on bank debt suffer less during the financial crisis; ② ownership concentration has a U-shaped relation to performance; ③ managerial ownership is positively related to Ch_Q in the SOE subsample; ④ firms that adopt reputable accounting firms perform better. It is noteworthy that this analysis engenders a positive and significant coefficient on *BSHARE*. Consistent with Baek et al. (2004) and Bai et al. (2004), this result provides weak evidence that less expropriations of minority shareholder wealth exist in firms that issue B-shares, and thereby must meet international accounting standards. Differently from Table 3.6, *BOARDSIZE* has an insignificant coefficient in this analysis.

3.5.3 Pre-crisis period results

This chapter argues that SOEs performed better during the financial crisis because of less severe financial constraints. This chapter also mentions that investors are more conscious of expropriation problems during a financial crisis when their expected returns are low (Mitton, 2002). If those ideas hold true, I should not find the same relation between the governance variables (*D_SOE*, *LSOWN*, *BANKR*, *MOWN*) and Ch_Q during economic boom periods. As a robustness check, this chapter conducts the same regression analyses for the change in Tobin's Q during a pre-crisis period. Following Ivashina and Scharfstein (2010), this chapter defines the pre-crisis period as August 2006 through July 2007.[①] In this analysis, year 2005 data is used for independent variables except for *STD*, which is computed using monthly stock price data from August 2005 to July 2006. This test also allows me to address causality problems. If the former results are produced from the opposite causal relations (e.g., well-performing SOEs tend to adopt high managerial ownership), I should find the same result for the pre-crisis period (see Table 3.7).

---

① Chinese Stock price indices continuously increased during the period.

Table 3.7 Regression results for the pre-crisis period

The table reports regression results of the change in Tobin's Q during the pre-crisis period: August 2006 to July 2007. The sample comprises Chinese firms listed on the Shanghai and Shenzhen Stock Exchanges. Year 2005 data are used for all independent variables except for STD, which is computed using monthly stock price data during the August 2005 to July 2006 period. Model 4 adopts only SOEs for investigation. Figures in parentheses are t-statistics. See Table 3.1 for definitions of variables.

	Model 1	Model 2	Model 3	Model 4
D_SOE	-0.26** (-2.15)	-0.27** (-2.19)	-0.26** (-2.14)	
BANKR	-1.82*** (-3.22)	-1.81*** (-3.19)	-1.63*** (-2.83)	-2.85*** (-4.52)
SOE*BANKR			-3.3E-07*** (-2.96)	
LSOWN	4.46*** (3.38)	4.4*** (3.31)	4.11*** (3.15)	5.37*** (3.52)
LSOWN²	-4.37*** (-3.47)	-4.37*** (-3.45)	-3.99*** (-3.19)	-5.75*** (-4.10)
MOWN	-0.41 (-0.58)	-7.01*** (-3.13)	-0.41 (-0.57)	-6.94*** (-2.72)
MOWN²		14.51*** (3.24)		
BOARDSIZE	-0.38 (-1.49)	-0.37 (-1.45)	-0.37 (-1.45)	-0.19 (-0.57)
INDBOARD	-0.48 (-0.38)	-0.53 (-0.42)	-0.48 (-0.38)	-0.62 (-0.38)
DUALITY	0.22 (1.40)	0.22 (1.40)	0.21 (1.34)	0.24 (1.19)
BIG_FOUR	-0.48** (-2.36)	-0.47** (-2.31)	-0.40* (-1.92)	-0.49** (-2.14)
BSHARE	-0.45*** (-2.94)	-0.46*** (-3.00)	-0.45*** (-2.92)	-0.44*** (-2.79)
LEV	-0.26* (-1.66)	-0.25* (-1.65)	-0.26 (-1.64)	-0.05 (-0.14)

Table3. 7(continued)

LIQUID	0.15** (2.35)	0.15** (2.35)	0.15** (2.36)	0.13* (1.69)
EXPORTR	-0.03** (-2.43)	-0.03** (-2.50)	-0.03*** (-2.63)	0.14 (0.46)
ROA	-0.13 (-0.24)	-0.11 (-0.21)	-0.17 (-0.30)	-1.29 (-0.93)
B_M	-0.01*** (-2.62)	-0.01*** (-2.65)	-0.01** (-2.35)	-0.01** (-2.27)
STD	2.32*** (3.32)	2.33*** (3.30)	2.24*** (3.25)	2.78*** (3.22)
LN_MVALUE	0.24*** (4.12)	0.24*** (4.12)	0.25*** (4.35)	0.28*** (4.15)
INDUSTRY	Yes	Yes	Yes	Yes
N	955	955	955	697
Adjusted R^2	0.14	0.15	0.15	0.17

  *** : Significant at the 1% level; ** : Significant at the 5% level; * : Significant at the 10% level.

  The pre-crisis period results (see Table 3.7) engender a negative coefficient on *D_SOE*, *BANKR*, and *SOE* * *BANKR*, which shows a sharp contrast to the former result, but is consistent with previous studies (Xu & Wang, 1999; Zhang et al., 2001; Sun & Tong, 2003; Gunasekarage et al., 2007). In unreported analyses, this chapter finds that SOEs that have bank debt perform significantly worse than non-SOEs without bank debt. *LSOWN* has an inverse-U shaped relation to the pre-crisis performance, which also contradicts the crisis period result. When I adopt the interaction term between *D_SOE* and *LSOWN* instead of the squared term of *LSOWN*, the interaction term has a negative and statistically significant coefficient at the 0.01 level. These conflicting results provide clear evidence of the two faces of state ownership. State ownership provides substantial credit to SOEs without any requirements on capital budgeting decisions; as a result, state ownership allows Chinese firms to pursue public interests and engenders over-investment problems in normal economic conditions in which firms suffer less from financial constraints (Bai et al., 2000; Dewenter & Malatesta, 2001; Firth et al., 2008; Khwaja & Mian, 2005). Once the financial market tightened as a result of the financial crisis, however, the positive aspect of state ownership (liquidity supply) created substantial values that prevailed against the negative effects. This chapter argues that state ownership makes firms' shareholder wealth more stable.

The pre-crisis period regression engenders a negative coefficient on *MOWN* for the SOE sample (Model 4). A U-shaped relationship was found between *MOWN* and *Ch_Q* for the entire sample, but the estimated coefficients suggest that for most sample companies, firm value decreases with managerial ownership. Table 3.7 also engenders a negative and significant coefficient on *BIG_FOUR*, which contradicts those of the crisis-period result. Those results suggest that corporate governance mechanisms mitigate the expropriation problem that becomes more evident during crisis periods. This chapter also argues that our main results are not derived from the opposite causal relation.

3.6 Conclusions

Chinese corporate governance has several special characteristics that are likely to engender serious agency conflicts. This chapter investigates the effect of Chinese corporate governance structure on the change in firm value during the global financial crisis. The underlying idea is that expropriation problems become more severe during crisis periods (Baek et al., 2004; Johnson et al., 2000; Mitton, 2002; Lemmon & Lins, 2003). Analyses of firm value during crisis periods also allow me to shed light on some aspects of corporate governance that are less evident during normal economic situations (Kuppuswamy & Villalonga, 2010).

Using data from 970 Chinese-listed firms, this chapter finds evidence that SOEs that rely on bank debt experience less deterioration in stock performance during the crisis period, while they experience poor performance during the pre-crisis period. Large shareholder ownership has a U-shaped relation to the crisis-period performance, which suggests that ownership concentration mitigates financial constraints and engenders expropriation problems. The Chapter argues that the state provides substantial credits to SOEs, allaying financing constraints during a crisis period while engendering overinvestment problems in normal economic conditions. State ownership has two faces; as a result, state-controlled firms show more stable stock performances. This chapter also finds that managerial ownership is positively associated with firm value changes for SOEs, when controlling for various firm characteristics. This result, which is consistent with the view that managerial ownership is effective in aligning managerial interests with those of minority shareholders, provides support for Li et al.'s (2007) finding while controlling for causality problems. In addition, firms with prestigious accounting auditors experienced small reductions in firm value during the global financial crisis. This result is consistent with the idea that better disclosure is associated with higher firm performance (Baek et al., 2004; Bushman & Smith, 2001; Diamond & Verrecchia, 1991; Glosten & Milgrom, 1985; Healy & Palepu, 2001; Hope & Thomas, 2008; Meek et al., 1995; Mitton, 2002). The results offer additional evidence that strong corporate governance plays an important role in mitigating the expropriations of minority shareholders.

The investigation offers some important implications for the literature. While previous studies stress a negative aspect of state ownership (Gunasekarage et al., 2007; Sun & Tong, 2003; Xu & Wang, 1999; Zhang et al., 2001), this chapter provides new evidence that state ownership has positive effects on firm value during a crisis period. Similarly, this chapter shows new evidence that bank debt has a positive effect on firm performance during a crisis period. This result, which stands in sharp contrast to previous findings (Baek et al., 2004; Kang & Stultz, 2000; Nogata et al., 2010), suggests that state-controlled banking systems effectively mitigate firms' financial constraints during financial crisis periods. Recent corporate governance studies stress that high levels of ownership by managers or families allows the expropriation of minority shareholder wealth (Leuz et al., 2009). In contrast, this chapter finds that extremely low managerial ownership engenders significant agency conflicts especially in firms that have strong controlling shareholders.

Although my empirical findings include several important implications for the corporate governance literature, there are several unsolved issues. What conditions make state ownership beneficial or detrimental to firm performance? Why is there a U-shaped relationship between equity ownership and firm value during a crisis? Do legal and cultural characteristics explain the positive effects of state ownership and bank loans on stock performance during a financial crisis?[①] Further study on those issues both from the theoretical and empirical approach is an important task for future research.

[①] Licht et al. (2005) argue that corporate governance research should incorporate national cultural characteristics as well as legal systems. Gleason et al. (2000) show that corporate capital structures that vary with culture affect firm performance. Shao et al. (2010) suggest that corporate policies are affected by managers and investors' subjective perception on agency problems as well as by the degree of agency conflicts.

4. Long-term stock performance following top executive turnover: Evidence from China

4.1 Introduction

It is commonly reported that forced managerial turnover is preceded by poor firm performance and is then followed by improved firm performance in countries with a strong legal system, which reflects the effectiveness of corporate control practices (Denis & Denis, 1995; Denis et al., 1997a; Huson et al., 2001; Huson et al., 2004; Kang & Shivdasani, 1995; McNeil et al., 2004). In countries with a weak legal system, however, the objective of management turnover could be different from that of countries with a strong legal system. Because poor investor rights protection is associated with high ownership concentration (La Porta et al., 1998, 2000a), top executive turnover tends to reflect the objectives of controlling shareholders rather than minority shareholders. As a result, the effect of management turnover on subsequent stock performance is potentially different from that in countries where a strong legal system is in place.

The Chinese corporate system, which provides weak legal protection for investors, offers a unique environment in which to address this issue.

Furthermore, the ownership structure is highly concentrated and the largest shareholder has much higher equity stakes than the second-largest shareholder (Chen et al., 2009; Firth et al., 2006a; Gul et al., 2010; Wang, 2005). In addition, most of the controlling shareholders are state owned, and tend to pursue non-performance objectives (social and/or political objectives) (Bai et al., 2000; Clarke, 2003; Dixit, 1997; Shleifer & Vishny, 1994, 1997). Importantly, most of the controlling shareholders and block-holders hold untradeable shares, and thus cannot achieve capital gains, which is not the case for minority shareholders who hold tradable shares. This characteristic of Chinese-listed firms implies that majority shareholders of Chinese listed firms may be less concerned with stock prices in the assessment of managerial performance. However, in 2005, the split-share reform launched by the Chinese Government converts untradeable shares into tradable shares (CSRC, 2005). On completion of the reform, shares held by controlling shareholders become tradable gradually. As a result, controlling shareholders, like minority shareholders, have the opportunity to realize capital gains by trading their shares. It is likely that firms that experience turnover after completion of the split-share reform are inclined to discipline CEOs in consideration of the CEOs' ability to improve stock price performance.

This chapter intends to explore whether top executive turnover serves as an effective mechanism in improving a company's stock performance among China's listed firms, and how split-share reform influences controlling shareholders' incentive to discipline their executive manager based on stock price. Before the split-share reform, the conflict of interest between controlling-minority shareholders in terms of capital gains was acute due to the concentrated and split-share ownership structure. In contrast, after completion of the split-share reform, as controlling shareholders have a chance to realize capital gains on the market through a maximization of stock prices to their own benefit, this reform potentially aligns the wealth implications of stock prices between controlling and minority shareholders. Therefore, CEO turnover may be sensitive to stock price movement and lead to significant improvement in stock performance following turnover. However, does executive turnover truly result in improvement in stock performance for all turnover firms after split-share reform? Controlling shareholders may need to retain control of the firm to provide insurance for outside investors, and also hold onto significant ownership as a commitment to limit the expropriation of minority shareholders even when their shares become tradable during the post-reform period.① Thus, shares held by controlling shareholders will be inherently less liquid (Cooper, 2008; Huang et al., 2011; La Porta et al., 2002). Therefore, controlling shareholders are not likely to pursue and achieve capital gains even after split-share reform.

As outside (minority) shareholders' wealth depends directly on stock performance among China's listed firms, it is important whether controlling shareholders have an incentive and the ability to exercise effective corporate control to improve stock performance. If controlling shareholders have weak incentive to discipline CEOs based on stock performance to maximize shareholders' wealth in the form of capital gain, this creates a divergence of interests between controlling and minority shareholders (Chang & Wong, 2004). In light of this, the question whether CEO turnover improves firm's stock performance should be of great interest to potential investors.

Previous studies focus exclusively on the pre-reform period, and examine the effectiveness of managerial turnover for China's listed firms.② Most of these studies investigate the sensitivity of turnover and performance (Conyon & He, 2011; Kato & Long, 2006a; Wang, 2010), measured by both accounting and stock performance. Regarding performance following managerial turnover, Chang and Wong (2009) examine the post-turnover performance of China's listed firms and find that there is an improvement in post-turnover accounting performance in loss-making firms. However, improvement in accounting performance does not necessarily mean improve-

---

① Hereafter, post-reform period means period after the completion of split-share reform.
② Hereafter, pre-reform period means period before the completion of split-share reform.

ment in stock performance among China's listed firms. It is possible that controlling shareholders have an incentive to maximize accounting performance subsequent to managerial turnover, and then pay a high dividend to meet their cash needs (Lee & Xiao, 2004; Lin et al., 2010; Tang & Luo, 2006). As a result, stock performance could still be poor following turnover, even though a company has rich growth opportunity, and accounting performance is good.① To the best of my knowledge, however, few studies address stock performance following managerial turnover for Chinese firms. As an exception, Kato and Long (2006b) examine CEO turnover of 634 listed firms from 1998 to 2002 and find that improvement in firm performance after the replacement of the CEO is greater for privately controlled firms than for state-controlled listed firms. However, they did not include post-reform turnovers in their sample. As this chapter has discussed, there is a big change in a controlling shareholder's incentive to discipline the CEO based on stock performance before and after reform; thus, post-reform turnovers tend to have different effects on subsequent stock performance.

In this chapter, as my sample period is quite recent (from 2001 to 2007), it allows me to investigate stock performance following managerial turnover during both pre-reform and post-reform periods, and present evidence on the different patterns of performance following managerial turnover for the two periods. In addition, this chapter analyzes the determinants of turnover-related firm stock performance changes, and provide further evidence on how split-share reform influences stock performance subsequent to executive turnover.

Using a sample of 666 CEO turnovers of Chinese listed firms for the period 2001–2007, this chapter documents that there is no improvement in stock performance after CEO turnover during the pre-reform period. However, in the post-reform period, there is a significant improvement in stock performance following CEO turnover in firms that have shown negative

---

① Minority shareholders prefer to have capital gains, because they are subject to 20% in income tax on cash dividends, whereas, in China, capital gains are tax-free.

shareholder returns, but there is no such improvement in firms that have shown non-negative returns. The post-reform result supports the hypothesis that controlling shareholders have an incentive to identify new managers who have the ability to improve performance, and also assess their new CEOs based on stock price in firms that have exhibited negative shareholder returns. In addition, our cross-sectional analysis indicates that turnover-related change in stock performance is positively related to CEO turnover in firms that have exhibited negative shareholder returns during the post-reform period, which provides consistent evidence. Finally, the regression results show that the percentage ownership of the controlling shareholder has a positive impact on turnover-related change in stock performance.

The rest of the chapter proceeds as follows. Section 2 discusses the hypotheses. Section 3 describes the sample selection procedure, data source, and variables. The empirical results are presented in Section 4, and Section 5 summarizes and concludes the chapter.

4.2 Hypotheses

Previous studies have shown that managerial turnover is associated with improved stock return (Kang & Shivdasani, 1995; Khorana, 2001; Huson et al., 2004; Hillier & McColgan, 2009). In China, listed firms typically have a dominant shareholder (Chen et al., 2009; Firth et al., 2006a; Gul et al., 2010; Wang, 2005). Furthermore, most majority shareholders hold either state shares or legal-person shares, which were not tradable before 2006 (CSRC, 2005). As controlling shareholders couldn't realize capital gains by trading their shares, they were less inclined to discipline CEOs based on stock price. Moreover, the government is often the controlling shareholder of listed firms and tends to sacrifice firm's economic performance to achieve social and political objectives (non-performance objectives) (Shleifer & Vishny, 1994, 1997; Dixit, 1997). As a result, state-controlled firms are likely to replace CEOs based on political/social achievement, and therefore provide managers with weak economic performance incentives. Thus, this unique ownership structure of China's listed firms will weaken or even eliminate stock performance improvement following top management turnover before completion of split-share reform. This chapter predicts that there is a small improvement in stock performance following CEO turnover during the pre-reform period (H1: *expropriation hypothesis*). However, during the post-reform period, controlling shareholders have the opportunity to sell their shares to achieve capital gains. As a result, controlling shareholders have the incentive to discipline CEOs based on stock performance, because stock price maximization will benefit them. These discussions naturally give rise to the prediction that CEO turnover is likely to result in improved stock performance during the post-reform period (H2a: *alignment hypothesis*).

As previous studies on the sensitivity of top management turnover to stock performance for China's listed firms show that privately controlled firms are more likely to replace the top executive manager based on market performance measures (Conyon & He, 2011; Kato & Long, 2006a), this chapter thus predicts that there is a greater likelihood of improved stock performance following CEO turnover for privately controlled firms than for state-owned enterprises (SOEs).

Regarding the impact of managerial turnover on subsequent stock performance after the completion of split-share reform, however, this chapter also can make an alternative hypothesis. Policy guidelines on split-share reform, issued by the CSRC, stated that the official objective of the reform was not to reduce state ownership, but rather to eliminate untradeable shares, and that in enterprises deemed strategic control will remain tightly in the hands of the government. Opinion exists from non-government institution that share the same view. In addition, some companies' reform proposals explicitly declared that the controlling shareholder would maintain controlling stakes in the company (Cooper, 2008). These facts imply that to retain their controlling power, many controlling shareholders would rarely sell their shares, even after the reform; as a result, their shares are inherently less liquid (Huang et al., 2011), and the incentive of controlling shareholders to improve stock performance following CEO turnover is still weak even after split-share reform. However, with the substantial increase in the proportion of tradable shares, the controlling shareholders of firms with extremely poor stock performance (negative shareholder returns) are likely to face great pressure from minority shareholders to improve performance, and thus attach more weight to improving stock performance (performance objective). They might tend to compensate minority investors for incurred losses as long as they are interested in continued external financing, which is especially true for China's listed firms because the Chinese economy is still growing and many listed firms have rich investment opportunities. Under these conditions, many controlling shareholders thus have the incentive to reverse a company's poor stock market performance by identifying managers with the ability to improve performance, and also assess new CEOs based on stock performance. Therefore, firms that have exhibited negative shareholder returns tend to have improved stock performance following turnover.

In contrast, firms that have exhibited non-negative shareholder returns, as the controlling shareholder does not face great pressure from the stock market to improve stock performance, attach less weight to improving stock performance and thus have weak incentive to discipline CEOs based on stock price performance; instead, many firms' controlling shareholder are likely to pursue a non-performance objective[①]. As a result, CEO turnovers result in little improvement in stock performance, and the stock's

---

[①] As mentioned in Chapter 1, firms controlled by the government have multiple and often conflicting objectives pursued by the state shareholders (Chang & Wong, 2009; Bai et al., 2000; Bai et al., 2006; Dixit, 1997). In addition, previous studies show that factors other than performance (e.g., social and political factors) also play an important role in determining managerial turnover in private firms (Fredrickson et al., 1988; Gibelman & Gelman, 2002; Shen & Cannella, 2002).

price is even likely to deteriorate due to the pursuit of non-performance objectives. Overall, most controlling shareholders have an incentive to discipline their CEOs based on financial performance when their shareholders are incurring financial losses. The result is improved stock performance following turnover for firms that have exhibited negative shareholder returns during the post-reform period (H2b: *different incentive of controlling shareholders hypothesis*).

4.3 Sample selection and data

4.3.1 Sample selection

To examine the impact of CEO turnover on subsequent stock performance, this chapter selects CEO turnover companies from non-financial firms listed on Shanghai Stock Exchange and the Shenzhen Stock Exchange during the period 1999—2007. To assess the effectiveness of corporate control exercised by controlling shareholders, this chapter needs to distinguish between forced and non-forced turnovers because only forced turnovers reflect shareholders' disciplinary efforts (Chang & Wong, 2009; Chi & Wang, 2009; Wang, 2010). Following Chang and Wong (2009), this chapter first excludes those samples for which the stated reasons are retirement, health (including death), corporate governance reform, and a change in controlling shareholders, and then excludes those cases that involved in legal disputes (see Table 4.1 for definitions of variables).

In line with previous studies (Chang & Wong, 2009), this chapter consolidates multiple CEO turnovers for a given firm in a given fiscal year. Thus, if a firm experiences two or more CEO turnovers in the same fiscal year, only the first turnover will be recorded. For the remaining turnovers, this chapter eliminates observations that CEOs were replaced within one year of being appointed because such replacements are less likely due to corporate control practices (Chang & Wong, 2009; Wang, 2010). This chapter also deletes those turnovers that experienced a CEO turnover within two years following their initial public offerings because Chinese IPOs tend to experience stock underperformance (Chan et al., 2004; Loughran & Ritter, 1995; Ritter, 1991). As this chapter intends to examine stock performance over a three-year period following CEO turnover, that the new CEO's tenure was less than three years are excluded.[①] Finally, this chapter requires that sample firms have at least one year of stock price data preceding the managerial turnover year and at least 36 months of stock price data following turnover; that is why this chapter ends the sample period at year 2007. This process yielded a final sample of 666 CEO turnovers among China's listed firms from 2001 to 2007.

Table 4.1   Definitions of variables

This table defines the study variables.	
Variables	Definitions
BHAR	Buy-and-hold abnormal returns.
SIZE	Market value of equity at the end of year prior to the CEO turnover.
B/M	Book value of equity divided by the market value of equity at the end of year prior to the CEO turnover.
SHR	Buy-and-hold returns from January to December during year prior to the CEO turnover.
SOE	State-owned enterprises, firms controlled by the state.
Non_SOE	Firms controlled by private.
N_SHR	Turnover samples exhibited negative annual buy-and-hold returns (SHR) over the year prior to the CEO turnover.
P_SHR	Turnover samples exhibited positive (non-negative) annual buy-and-hold returns (SHR) over the year prior to the CEO turnover.

---

① It will take a few years for a new manager to do many things to maximize shareholder value after he/she is appointed; furthermore, news of new appointments will increase stock price.

Table 4.1 (continued)

REFORM	Dummy variable that takes the value of one for firms that exhibited managerial turnover after their completion of split-share reform.
D_SHR	Dummy variable that takes the value of one for firms that exhibited negative annual buy-and-hold returns (SHR) over the year prior to the CEO turnover.
STATE	Dummy variable that takes the value of one for firms in which the controlling shareholder is the government.
BOARDSIZE	Natural logarithm of the number of directors at year prior to the CEO turnover.
INDBOARD	Number of independent directors divided by the number of total board members at year prior to the CEO turnover.
CONCENTRATION	The percentage of shares owned by the largest shareholder at year prior to the CEO turnover.
GROWTH	Growth in assets in the year prior to the CEO turnover.
$ROA(t-1)$	Return on assets in year t−1.
$ROA(t-2)$	Return on assets in year t−2.

This chapter obtains data on CEO turnover, corporate governance data, financial data, and monthly stock price data from the China Corporate Governance Research Database (CCGRD) developed by GTA Information Technology Co.[①]

Panel A of Table 4.2 presents the distribution of our sample by calendar year. Panel B reports the distribution of sample by stated reasons. The results show that about 46% of samples disclose the reason for replacing the CEO as change of job, which is consistent with the view that there is a lack of transparency about the true reasons for top management turnover in China's listed firms because of the culture of harmony and saving face in social relationships (Firth et al., 2006b). Panel C presents the industry dis-

---

[①] The CCGRD database covers information regarding senior management changes and other corporate governance data from year 1999 onwards. However, we identify only CEO turnover samples that meet our selection requirements from year 2001.

tribution of sample firms. It is noteworthy that most of the samples are within the manufacturing sector (58%).

Table 4.2　　　　Sample distribution

This table presents the sample distribution by CEO turnover year (Panel A), stated reasons (Panel B) and industry (Panel C). The sample consists of 666 firms that experienced CEO turnover between 2001 and 2007.

Panel A: Distribution by CEO turnover year

CEO turnover year	Number of turnover samples	Percent (%)
2001	78	11.71
2002	101	15.17
2003	102	15.32
2004	98	14.71
2005	114	17.12
2006	107	16.07
2007	66	9.91
Total	666	100

Panel B: Distribution by stated reasons

Stated reasons	Number of turnover samples	Percent (%)
Change of job	306	45.95
Contract expiration	150	22.52
Resignation	125	18.77
Dismissal	24	3.6
Personal reasons	20	3
Completion of acting duties	13	1.95
No reason given	28	4.2
Total	666	100

Panel C: Distribution by industry

Industry	Number of turnover samples	Percent (%)
Agriculture, fishing, and stockraising	12	1.8
Mining	8	1.2
Manufacturing	389	58.4

Table4. 2(continued)

Electricity, gas, and water	25	3.75
Construction	11	1.65
Transportation and warehousing	29	4.35
IT	41	6.15
Wholesale and retail	53	7.95
Real estate	27	4.05
Social service	25	3.75
Media	6	0.9
Comprehensive	40	6.01
Total	666	100

4.3.2 Measure of turnover-related stock performance change

To measure turnover-related long-term stock performance change subsequent to managerial turnover, this chapter matches sample firms with a non-turnover benchmark firm having similar ex ante characteristics of stock return in the financial year prior to turnover, but with no turnover occurring in the event year and in the three years preceding the turnover (Chang & Wong, 2009; Wang, 2010). Jegadeesh and Titman (1993) document persistence in stock returns, which Fama and French (1996) are unable to explain well using factors related to firm size and book-to-market ratio. Carhart (1997) finds that persistence results from an omitted factor explaining equity returns, the momentum effect described by Jegadeesh and Titman (1993). Moreover, Lyon et al. (1999) find that the test statistics are all mis-specified in their pre-event return sub-samples and recommend matching the samples to firms with similar pre-event returns as well as size and B/M. Therefore, this chapter employs three-dimensional matching (size, B/M and past return matching) in the analysis. This chapter chooses as a matched firm the non-turnover company that is closest to the managerial turnover firm in Fama and French's (1992, 1993) size and book-to-market factors, and Carhart's momentum factor in stock returns.

As the three-dimensional matching method requires that the matched sample with similar past stock performance to the managerial turnover sample, it can yield well-specified test statistics (Lyon et al., 1999), and also controls the price momentum effect (Carhart, 1997; Jegadeesh & Titman, 1993); in addition, this method can avoid observed performance improvement due to potential mean reversion of the stock market performance time series (Balvers et al., 2000; Campbell & Shiller, 1988; Fama & French, 1988; Khorana, 2001; Poterba & Summers, 1988). Therefore, this method can provide useful insight in determining whether the turnover of CEOs is truly a value-generating activity in terms of stock performance in China's listed firms.

In the three-dimensional matching method, for year t, I first divided all firms (turnover firms and non-turnover benchmark firms that had not experienced turnover in the event year and in the three years preceding the turnover) into four groups by size. Within each size group, I ranked firms according to B/M ratio and sorted them into four B/M sub-groups, and then selected as a matched company the non-turnover firm in the same size and B/M group closest shareholder returns to the turnover firm over the past year.

After identifying a unique matching firm for each turnover sample firm, I subtracted the buy-and-hold returns of the matched firm from the corresponding holding period return for the managerial turnover firm. This is referred to as buy-and-hold abnormal return (*BHAR*); the matched firm's buy-and-hold return (*BHR*) is used as a benchmark return. Barber and Lyon (1997) and Lyon et al. (1999) argue that *BHARs* are important because they「precisely measure investor experience.」I believe *BHARs* will serve as an appropriate performance indicator in the Chinese stock market, where over 90% of investors are individuals.

This chapter computes 12-month, 24-month, and 36-month *BHARs* after the managerial turnover by using the following calculation method (hereafter denoted by $BHAR_{12}$, $BHAR_{24}$, and $BHAR_{36}$, respectively).

$$BHAR_{it} = \prod_{t=1}^{T}(1+R_{i,t}) - \prod_{t=1}^{T}(1+R_{benchmark,t}),$$
$$T \in (12,24,36),$$

Where $R_{i,t}$ is the monthly stock return of firm i in month t, $R_{benchmark,t}$ is the monthly stock return of firm i's benchmark firm in month t. This chapter defines month 1 as the month after the firm's managerial turnover. This chapter computes $R_{i,t}$ as

$$R_{i,t} = \frac{P_{i,t}-P_{i,t-1}+D_{i,t}}{P_{i,t-1}}$$

$P_{i,t}$ is the closing price of firm i's stock at month t. $D_{i,t}$ is the dividend payment of firm i in month t. The computation for $R_{benchmark,t}$ is the same.

4.4 Empirical results

4.4.1 Stock performance following CEO turnover

To test the consequence of CEO turnover on subsequent stock performance, Table 4.3 reports mean and median long-term stock performance following CEO turnover. Panel A and Panel B present results for pre-reform and post-reform turnovers, respectively. In Panel A, all the turnover-related performance changes for the entire sample are not positive and significant. In Panel B, the consequence of post-reform turnover is similar to that shown in Panel A, for the entire sample, there is no improvement in stock performance following CEO turnovers. To test the possibility that non-SOEs show improved stock performance following CEO turnover while SOEs do not. This chapter also presents stock performance following turnover separately for SOEs and non-SOEs in Table 4.3. The results show there is still no improvement in stock performance following turnover for the non-SOE as well as the SOE samples in both Panel A and Panel B.

Table 4.3 Long-term stock performance following CEO turnover

Table 4.3 presents the mean and median long-term stock performance following CEO turnover in Chinese firms. Means and medians are tested against zero by t-statistic and Wilcoxon signed rank test respectively. This chapter matches sample firms with a non-turnover control firm according to size, book-to-market ratio and past stock return over the year prior to the CEO turnover, and the buy-and-hold abnormal return (BHAR) is the difference between the turnover sample and matched firm' BHRs. Panel A and Panel B reports results for firms experience CEO turnover before and after split-share reform, respectively. T-test statistics and Z-statistics are in parentheses.

Type of turnover	No. Observations	12 Mean BHAR	12 Median BHAR	24 Mean BHAR	24 Median BHAR	36 Mean BHAR	36 Median BHAR
Panel A Before split-share reform							
all turnover	522	0.034 (1.207)	0.006 (0.626)	−0.022 (−0.299)	0.026 (1.148)	−0.061 (−0.659)	0.032 (0.002)
SOE	419	0.018 (0.603)	0.012 (0.452)	0.003 (0.045)	0.040* (1.814)	−0.068 (−0.654)	0.042 (0.495)
non-SOE	103	0.101 (1.312)	−0.009 (0.421)	−0.126 (−0.641)	−0.041 (−1.109)	−0.033 (−0.160)	−0.071 (−0.941)
Panel B After split-share reform							
all turnover	144	0.107 (0.778)	−0.035 (−0.327)	0.094 (1.065)	−0.019 (−0.104)	0.087 (0.622)	0.093 (1.015)
SOE	103	0.142 (0.853)	−0.016 (−0.003)	.130 (1.310)	−0.002 (0.332)	0.069 (0.469)	0.071 (0.615)
non-SOE	41	0.021 (0.085)	−0.134 (−0.525)	0.004 (0.023)	−0.078 (−0.667)	0.134 (0.405)	0.110 (0.875)

***: Significant at the 1% level; **: Significant at the 5% level; *: Significant at the 10% level

Overall, the results of Table 4.3 indicate that turnovers did not result in improved stock performance during both the pre-reform and post-reform periods. The result of the pre-reform period in Panel A is consistent with the expropriation hypothesis (H1); and controlling shareholders do not discipline their CEOs based on stock price due to their holding untradeable shares and the pursuit of non-performance objectives during the pre-reform period. However, this result of Panel B does not support the alignment hypothesis (H2a) for post-reform turnovers. This chapter interprets this as controlling shareholders having a weak incentive to reduce ownership and pursue capital gains due to inherently less liquid shares they hold (Cooper, 2008; Huang et al., 2011; La Porta et al., 2002).

To examine the hypothesis of different incentives of controlling shareholder during the post-reform period (H2b), this chapter decomposes the sample of managerial turnover based on the company's annual shareholder returns (SHR) during year t−1; firms that exhibited negative (non-negative) SHR are placed in the N_SHR (P_SHR) sample.[①] This chapter separately examines the improvement in stock performance following managerial turnover for N_SHR sub-sample and P_SHR sub-sample in Table 4.4. For the entire sample, the subsequent performance changes of the negative SHR sample (N_SHR) are positive over all of the three investment periods. The mean and median values in the 12-month investment period and mean value in the 24-month investment period are positive and significant at the 5% level, and the median values in the 24-month and 36-month investment period are marginally positive, while the post-turnover performance of the non-negative SHR sample (P_SHR) is negative in all corresponding periods; the mean and median value during the 12-month investment period are even significant. Moreover, the economic magnitude of the improvement in stock performance following CEO turnover in firms that have exhibited negative shareholder returns is large; all the mean and median BHARs are above 0.318, except the median value during the 24-month investment period. These results for the entire sample are generally consistent with the different incentive of controlling shareholder hypothesis (H2b); stock performance improves following turnover for firms that have exhibited negative shareholder returns during the post-reform period.

[①] Throughout this Chapter, we denote Year −1 as the year before the company experienced the CEO turnover.

Table 4.4 Long-term stock performance following CEO turnover during post-reform period

Table 4.4 presents the mean and median post-turnover long-term stock performance separately for firms exhibited negative and non-negative (positive) performance after split-share reform. Means and medians are tested against zero by t-statistic and Wilcoxon signed rank test respectively. This chapter matches sample firms with a non-turnover control firm according to size, book-to-market ratio and past stock return over the year prior to the CEO turnover, and the buy-and-hold abnormal return (BHAR) is the difference between the turnover sample and matched firm' BHRs. N_SHR (P_SHR) samples comprise turnover firms exhibited negative (positive) annual buy-and-hold returns (SHR) over the year prior to the CEO turnover. T-test statistics and Z-statistics are in parentheses.

Type of turnover		No. Observations	Time period (month)					
			12		24		36	
			Mean BHAR	Median BHAR	Mean BHAR	Median BHAR	Mean BHAR	Median BHAR
all turnover	N_SHR	57	0.791***	0.463***	0.449**	0.090*	0.318	0.341*
			(2.862)	(2.832)	(2.627)	(1.800)	(1.291)	(1.784)
	P_SHR	87	-0.340***	-0.148***	-0.137	-0.061*	-0.063	-0.103
			(-2.851)	(-3.009)	(-1.581)	(-1.710)	(-0.378)	(-0.495)
SOE	N_SHR	35	0.932**	0.461**	0.693***	0.386***	0.406	0.516**
			(2.220)	(2.263)	(3.249)	(2.637)	(1.527)	(1.963)
	P_SHR	68	-0.283**	-0.100**	-0.090	-0.043	-0.077	-0.153
			(-2.084)	(-1.983)	(-0.896)	(-1.029)	(-0.409)	(-0.866)

***: Significant at the 1% level; **: Significant at the 5% level; *: Significant at the 10% level

In Table 4.4, when I examine stock performance following turnover only for the SOEs sub-sample, CEO turnovers in firms that have exhibited negative shareholder returns (N_SHR) generate positive BHARs in all investment periods, and all BHARs, except the mean value in the 36-month investment period, are significant and economically large (ranging from 0.386 to 0.932). As SOEs face great pressure from the stock market to improve performance after their stocks have performed extremely poorly (negative stock returns), SOEs are likely to pursue stock performance objective rather than non-performance objectives. This result should also be true for non-SOEs, which are more likely to discipline top executive managers based on performance than their counterparts of state-controlled firms. In unreported results, this chapter also examines the subsequent stock performance of non-SOEs. All the turnover-related performance changes of the negative *SHR* sample (*N_SHR*), except median value in the 24-month investment period, are positive but not significant. A possible reason is that the sample size of 22 is too small, and more data needs to be collected before conducting the analyses.

Overall, the positive and significant improvement following CEO turnover in SOEs that have exhibited negative shareholder returns indicates that SOEs, which typically tend to pursue non-performance objectives and are not likely to discipline their CEO based on stock performance, reverse the company's poor stock market performance by replacing their top executive manager after split-share reform. Therefore, the results of Table 4.4 are consistent with the different incentive of the controlling shareholder hypothesis (H2b), and suggest that most controlling shareholders have an incentive to identify managers with the ability to improve performance and to assess their new CEOs based on stock performance when their shareholders are incurring financial losses after split-share reform.

4.4.2 Cross-sectional determinants of turnover-related change in stock performance

To examine the impacts of split-share reform on long-term stock performance following CEO turnovers after controlling for various factors, this chapter conducts a multivariate regression analysis that adopts *BHARs* under the three-dimensional matching method as a dependent variable. This chapter adopts the interaction term between *REFORM* (a dummy variable equal to one for firms that replace their CEO after completion of split-share reform) and *D_SHR* (a dummy variable that takes the value of one for firms that exhibited negative annual buy-and-hold returns over the year t−1) to identify the firms that experience CEO turnovers during the post-reform period and which show negative shareholder returns (*D_SHR* * *REFORM*). As documented in Section 4.4.1, this chapter predicts that *D_SHR* * *RE-*

FORM is positively associated with turnover-related changes.

Huson et al. (2004) argue that examining the relations between the characteristics of monitoring mechanisms and the change in firm performance following CEO turnover can provide direct evidence of the impact of these governance characteristics on the quality of CEO selections. This chapter includes several monitoring mechanism variables that potentially influence turnover-related change in stock performance. Individual investors have weak incentives to invest in monitoring and to exert influence over key corporate decisions when ownership is dispersed (Fama & Jensen, 1983a; Jensen & Meckling, 1976), while concentrated share ownership can mitigate the free-rider problem and make management accountable for performance (Kang & Shivdasani, 1995). In the regression this chapter uses the percentage of shares owned by the largest shareholder as a measure of ownership concentration (*CONCENTRATION*). In order to examine the effect of ownership type of controlling shareholder, this chapter constructs a dummy variable equal to one for firms in which the controlling shareholder is the government (STATE), which tends to have certain non-performance objectives (social and political objectives) that they impose on top management (Bai et al., 2000; Clarke, 2003). Michael (1988) and Borokhovich et al. (1996) suggest that performance improvement following management turnover could be related to the extent of outsider representation on the board of directors. In this chapter, I measure board size as the natural logarithm of the number of directors (*BOARDSIZE*); and board independence is defined as the number of independent directors divided by the number of board members (*INDBOARD*). Following the research of Jenter et al. (2010), this chapter also includes *SIZE*, *B/M*, and asset growth (*GROWTH*) in year $t-1$, and accounting return in year $t-1$ and $t-2$. See Table 4.1 for definitions of the variables.

In the regression, following Huson et al. (2004), the two-step method described by Heckman (1979) is used to obtain consistent estimates. Results for both the binomial probit and OLS regression are reported in Table

4. 5. The probit regressions provide evidence on the predictors of survival of firms that experience CEO turnover, but are estimated principally to obtain the inverse Mill's ratio (IML) value used in the OLS regressions. In the OLS regressions, this chapter winsorizes the dependent variables at the 1st and 99th percentile values. $BHAR_{12}$, $BHAR_{24}$, and $BHAR_{36}$ are regressed on the above-mentioned independent variables, as well as IML. When the necessary independent variables are not available, the observation is deleted from the analysis.

Table 4. 5 Sample selection models of turnover-related long-term stock performance change

This table reports the results of sample selection models, estimated as described by Heckman (1979), in which the dependent variable for the probit regression equals one if the firm survives as an independent entity for 36 months after the CEO turnover and zero otherwise. The sample consists of CEO turnover during the 2001–2007 periods. The OLS regression is estimated using only data for firms that survived 36 months. The dependent variable for the OLS regression equals the buy-and-hold abnormal return (BHAR) in investment period. IML is the inverse Mills ratio. All models included industry dummy and year dummy; however, results are not reported. Standard errors are reported in parentheses. See Table 4. 1 for definitions of variables.

	Probit regression	OLS regression		
	Firm retains independent	Model 1 ($BHAR_{12}$)	Model 2 ($BHAR_{24}$)	Model 3 ($BHAR_{36}$)
D_SHR	−0.32*(0.19)	−0.08(0.12)	−0.24(0.22)	−0.24(0.40)
REFORM		−0.87***(0.19)	−0.75**(0.34)	−0.30(0.59)
D_SHR * REFORM		0.93***(0.20)	0.76**(0.35)	0.29(0.61)
STATE	0.19(0.12)	−0.03(0.08)	0.07(0.15)	0.04(0.28)
BOARDSIZE	−0.31(0.24)	0.25*(0.14)	0.14(0.27)	0.28(0.50)
INDBOARD	−1.53*(0.82)	−0.23(0.56)	−0.44(1.02)	0.32(1.86)
CONCENTRATION	0.42(0.35)	0.15(0.21)	0.75**(0.38)	1.45**(0.70)
SIZE	0.05(0.08)	−0.00(0.04)	−0.01(0.09)	0.01(0.16)
B/M	0.22(0.18)	0.07(0.13)	−0.02(0.24)	0.23(0.44)
GROWTH	0.51**(0.24)	−0.05(0.06)	0.02(0.12)	0.20(0.22)
ROA(t−1)	0.09(0.24)	−0.16(0.24)	0.72*(0.41)	1.03(0.71)
ROA(t−2)	1.02**(0.42)	−0.10(0.46)	1.06(0.82)	2.23(1.44)

Table4.5(continued)

Industry dummy	Yes			
Year dummy	Yes			
Constant	−0.29(1.26)	−0.20(0.98)	−0.95(1.78)	−3.42(3.20)
IML		0.02(0.61)	0.99(1.08)	2.74(1.87)
N-total	839			
N-remain independent		658	658	658

*** : Significant at the 1% level; ** : Significant at the 5% level; * : Significant at the 10% level

In Table 4.5, the OLS regression shows that when I adopt $BHAR_{12}$ and $BHAR_{24}$ as dependent variables in Model 1 and Model 2, the estimated coefficient of $D\_SHR * REFORM$ is positive and significant at the 1% level and the 5% level respectively, while Model 3 adopted $BHAR_{36}$ as a dependent variable to engender a positive coefficient, though it is not statistically significant. The results indicate that, after completion of split-share reform in firms that have exhibited extremely poor stock performance (negative shareholder return), managerial turnover tends to improve stock market performance.

In contrast, these OLS regression analyses engender a negative and significant coefficient on REFORM in Model 1 and Model 2. After reform, the other block-holders' shares became tradable. These block-holders are also likely to be sophisticated investors. When firms exhibit non-negative shareholder return, and relatively many firms' controlling shareholders have weak incentive to identify a new manager with the ability to improve performance or to assess their new CEO based on stock performance, instead, they are likely to pursue a non-performance objective and also to extract private benefits at the expense of outsider investors. As a result, the secondary stock market tends to incorporate the expropriation of minority shareholders, and stock performance following turnover is likely to deteriorate.

Overall, the result of the OLS regression provides consistent evidence on different incentives of controlling shareholders in firms to exercise CEO turnover during the post-reform period. After the completion of split-share reform, controlling shareholders in many firms that have exhibited negative shareholder returns tend to pursue performance objective, and have an incentive to discipline their CEOs based on the stock price.

Regarding the corporate governance variable, only *CONCENTRATION* has a positive and significant coefficient in Model 2 and Model 3, while there is a positive but not significant coefficient in Model 1. As concentrated share ownership can mitigate the free-rider problem, it has a positive impact on turnover-related performance change. This chapter does not find evidence that *BOARDSIZE* and *INDBOARD* have a significant impact on long-term stock performance following CEO turnover. As the controlling shareholder has huge influence on the appointment of board member in Chinese listed firms, such boards do not effectively monitor management to be accountable for stock performance on behalf of minority shareholders.

4.5 Conclusions

To examine the consequences of managerial turnover of Chinese listed firms and provide complementary evidence on the quality of corporate control in China's listed firms, this chapter estimates stock performance change following CEO turnover after controlling the characteristics of stock returns. The results show that CEO turnover during the pre-reform period results in no improvement in stock performance; however, in the post-reform period, there is a significant improvement in stock performance following CEO turnover in firms that have exhibited negative shareholder returns, but no such improvement in firms that have exhibited non-negative returns. The post-reform results support the different incentive of the controlling shareholder hypothesis (H2b), that many controlling shareholders have an incentive to pursue stock performance objective by top executive turnover when firms have exhibited negative shareholder returns during the post-reform period.

CEO turnover in firms that record poor stock performance is truly a value-generating activity for minority shareholders during the post-reform period.

This chapter also investigates the cross-sectional determinants of turnover-related stock performance change, and finds that stock performance change is positively related to the presence of negative shareholder returns of firms experiencing CEO turnover in the post-reform period, which provides consistent evidence on different incentives of controlling shareholders after reform. Finally, this chapter finds that turnover samples with a high percentage of controlling shareholders tend to exhibit high improvement in subsequent stock performance.

The study of top executive turnover for China's firms also provides a better understanding of the impact of split-share reform on investor protection and the agency problem in China's listed firms. After split-share reform, many controlling shareholders still have weak incentive to discipline the executive manager based on stock performance except in firms whose stock has performed extremely poorly (negative shareholder return), because they desire to maintain their control of listed firms and have a weak incentive to pursue capital gain even when their shares become tradable.

One weakness of this chapter is including a small sample of companies experiencing CEO turnover after the completion of split-share reform; therefore, the finding during the post-reform period needs further testing when a large sample become available.

5. Controlling shareholder, split-share structure reform and cash dividend payments in China

5.1 Introduction

Previous studies have suggested that controlling shareholders expropriate minority shareholder wealth by exerting influential power on corporate dividend policy (Easterbrook, 1984; Faccio et al., 2001; Jensen, 1986; Gugler & Yurtoglu, 2003; La Porta et al., 2000b). This problem is also evident in China because China's listed firms have highly concentrated ownership structures where the largest shareholder has much higher equity stakes than does the second largest shareholder (Chen, 2009; Cheng et al., 2009; Firth et al., 2006a; Gul et al., 2010; Wang, 2005). In addition, China had a unique split-share system in which shares of listed firms were split into two categories: non-publicly tradable shares (NPTS) and publicly tradable shares (PTS) (Huang et al., 2011; Li, Wang, Cheung & Jiang, 2009; Wei & Xiao, 2009; Yeh et al., 2009). The split share system is likely to engender expropriation problems in addition to a concentrated ownership structure (Jiang et al., 2010; Zou et al., 2008). The present chapter principally explores the expropriation problem associated with cash dividend payments in China's listed companies.

Importantly, the China Securities Regulatory Commission (CSRC) launched a split-share structure reform program in 2005, with the aim of eliminating NPTS that were a potential source of expropriation problems (CSRC, 2005). The ownership structures of China's listed companies showed a substantial change after the reform; at the end of 2009, approximately 80% of NPTS were converted to tradable shares. Previous studies have suggested that the non-tradability of shares was a main determinant of Chinese controlling shareholders' preferences for cash dividends (Cheng et al., 2009; Huang et al., 2011; Lin et al., 2010; Wei & Xiao, 2009). Accordingly, the substantial reduction in the proportion of NPTS must affect the cash dividend policy.

During the stock reform process, Chinese firms also experienced a decline in ownership concentration that potentially changed their dividend policy. A majority of reforming firms offered free bonus shares to existing PTS holders as compensation from NPTS holders (Cooper, 2008; Bortolotti & Beltratti, 2007; Yeh et al., 2009). The free bonus share substantially decreased the proportion of NPTS and the percentage ownership by controlling shareholders. However, to the best of my knowledge, little academic attention has been paid to the impact of split-share structure reform on Chinese corporate dividend policy. Additionally, split-share reform, launched by the state, is an exogenous shock for individual firms; therefore, the reduction in NPTS and ownership concentration that is associated with the reform provides a good opportunity to investigate the effects on cash dividend payments. The current research environment was close to a natural experiment and allowed us to avoid endogeneity problems.[①] Therefore, this chapter takes this advantage and reexamines the relationship between NPTS, ownership concentration, and cash dividend payments in China. In addition, the

---

① For example, firms that pay high dividends are likely to maintain a high proportion of NPTS held by the controlling shareholders.

reduction in ownership concentration via the reform process was relatively small compared to that of NPTS. This fact allows me to investigate, separately, the effect of NPTS on dividend policy and the impact of concentrated ownership structures.

This chapter computes the differences in cash dividend payments for individual Chinese companies before and after the stock reform and compares this data to the changes in NPTS and the percentage of ownership of the largest shareholder. The empirical evidence indicates that the change in cash dividends was not significantly related to the change in NPTS; however was associated with the change in the percentage of ownership of the controlling shareholder. Therefore, this chapter argues that inherent illiquidity of stocks of the controlling shareholders is a most important factor as it related to the controlling shareholder's preference for cash dividends. Previous studies have argued that NPTS has a significant relationship with dividend payouts in China (Cheng et al., 2009; Huang et al., 2011; Lin et al., 2010; Wei & Xiao, 2009). However, my evidence suggests that NPTS, *per se*, does not affect Chinese corporate dividend policy. A possible interpretation of previous findings is that, before the split-share structure reform, there was an automatic correlation between the proportion of NPTS and percentage ownership of controlling shareholders because the controlling shareholders owned NPTS; as a result, there was a positive correlation between cash dividends and NPTS. My data also indicates that, after the reform, the percentage of ownership by controlling shareholders had a significant cross-sectional positive relation to the absolute level of cash dividends. In contrast, this chapter does not find any significant associations between the proportion of NPTS over the total outstanding shares and absolute cash dividend level. This result provides further evidence that the controlling shareholders still prefer cash dividends because of the inherent illiquidity of their shares.

This research makes important contributions to the existing literature. For example, previous studies have argued that stock non-tradability engenders agency problems regarding dividend policy between controlling and minority shareholders (Cheng et al., 2009; Huang et al., 2011; Lee & Xiao, 2004; Lin et al., 2010; Lv & Zhou, 2005; Tang & Luo, 2006; Wei & Xiao, 2009; Yuan, 2001). To the best of my knowledge, this is the first research to demonstrate that ownership concentration is more relevant to corporate dividend policy than to non-tradability of shares. Specifically, as long as controlling shareholders need to provide insurance for outside investors, their shares will be less liquid and controlling shareholders will prefer cash dividends. Importantly, this chapter presents the evidence in a research environment that does not suffer from endogeneity problems to the extent that previous studies have.

The remainder of this chapter is organized as follows. Section 2 presents background information and the hypotheses. Section 3 presents the sample selection procedure and data. In Section 4 I present the empirical results. Section 5 discusses further analyses. Section 6 summarizes and concludes the current research.

5.2 Hypotheses

Previous studies have argued that, in countries with strong investor protection, dividends serve as an effective instrument for mitigating agency problems between controlling and minority shareholders (Faccio et al., 2001; Gugler & Yurtoglu, 2003; La Porta et al., 2000b). However, the dividend expropriation hypothesis in China is distinct from other countries as cash dividends exacerbate expropriation problems between controlling and minority shareholders (Cheng et al., 2009; Huang et al., 2011; Lee & Xiao, 2004; Lin et al., 2010; Lv & Zhou, 2005; Tang & Luo, 2006; Wei & Xiao, 2009; Yuan, 2001). Additionally, China has a unique split-share ownership structure in which shares of listed firms are divided into NPTS and PTS (Huang et al., 2011; Li, Wang, Cheung & Jiang, 2009;

Wei & Xiao, 2009; Yeh et al., 2009). Controlling shareholders, who typically hold NPTS, cannot achieve capital gains because of the non-tradability of their shares. Rather, only cash dividends provide controlling shareholders with an opportunity to achieve returns on their shareholdings (Cheng et al., 2009; Huang et al., 2011; Lee & Xiao, 2004; Lin et al., 2010; Tang & Luo, 2006; Wei & Xiao, 2009).[①] Importantly, PTS holders are subject to 20% in income tax on cash dividends, whereas, in China, capital gains are tax-free.

Further, previous studies have demonstrated that PTS holders prefer stock dividends to cash dividends (Cheng et al., 2009; Huang et al., 2011; Wei & Xiao, 2009; Yuan, 2001). In addition, the Chinese economy is still in the growing stage and many listed firms have rich investment opportunities. In this environment, high cash dividend payouts potentially engender underinvestment problems and destroy the minority shareholder value (Lin et al., 2010). This suggests that the controlling shareholder's preference for cash dividends would engender expropriation problems in China. Zhou and Lv (2008) present a good case study which indicates that cash dividend payment is excessive in China's listed firms, and controlling shareholders expropriate small shareholders' wealth through the largest dividends distribution (see Appendix 2). As such, research has also provided evidence that the level of cash dividends is significantly and positively related to the proportion of NPTS (Cheng et al., 2009; Huang et al., 2011; Lin et al., 2010; Wei & Xiao, 2009).

As mentioned, CSRC launched the split-share structure reform program in 2005, with the aim of converting NPTS into PTS. The reform substantially decreased the proportion of NPTS and the percentage ownership by controlling shareholders. Previous studies have shown that NPTS holders (typically controlling shareholders) prefer cash dividends because of the non-tradability of their shares. This finding naturally gives rise to a predic-

---

[①] Stock repurchases are not allowed in China.

tion that Chinese firms decreased cash dividends before and after the reform, which substantially decreased NPTS. Importantly, the split-share reform is an exogenous shock and firms were forced to reduce NPTS. Therefore, this reform allowed me to investigate the effect of NPTS on dividend payments and avoid endogeneity problems.

H1: *Chinese firms reduced cash dividends before and after the split-share structure reform. The change in cash dividends is positively related to the change in the proportion of NPTS over total outstanding shares.*

As mentioned, the free bonus share issued reduced ownership concentration of Chinese firms. The largest shareholder ownership declined from approximately 43% in 2004, to about 35% by the end of 2009. Conversely, policy guidelines, issued by CSRC, stated that the official objective of the reform was not to reduce state ownership, rather to eliminate NPTS. In addition, some companies' reform proposals explicitly declared that the controlling shareholder would maintain the controlling stakes in the company (Cooper, 2008). These facts imply that controlling shareholders would retain their power even after the reform; the concentrated ownership structure is still a distinct feature of Chinese corporate governance. Huang et al. (2011) point out that as long as there is a need for large co-investors to provide insurance for outside investors, shares held by controlling shareholders will be less liquid and controlling shareholders will prefer cash dividends. Additionally, controlling shareholders rarely sell their shares to retain controlling power and, as a result, their shares are inherently less liquid. In addition, many investors are likely to follow buy-and-sell behaviors of those controlling shareholders who are well-informed about the company.[①] Therefore, it is difficult for controlling shareholders to sell substantial shares because this action would be accompanied by significant stock price

---

[①] In China, controlling shareholder whose stake exceeds 5% of the equity outstanding has to disclose increases or decreases of his stake, if the change exceeds 5% (Guidelines for controlling shareholders, de facto controllers of Listed Companies, issued by Shanghai Stock Exchange).

fluctuations. This suggests that controlling shareholders are likely to prefer cash dividends because the inherent illiquidity of their shares prevents them from achieving capital gains.

Dividend payments in China are likely to be affected by ownership concentration and the non-tradability of shares (Faccio et al., 2001; Gugler & Yurtoglu, 2003; Maury & Pajuste, 2002). Indeed, Lee & Xiao (2004), Lin et al. (2010), and Tang and Luo (2006) found that Chinese firms with concentrated ownership structures tended to pay higher cash dividends to meet the cash needs of the largest shareholders. However, they interpreted their results as evidence of an effect of share non-tradability on dividend policy. The present chapter attempts to disentangle the effect of ownership concentration from that of share non-tradability. Specifically, this chapter proposes an alternative hypothesis regarding the channel through which the split-share reform affects cash dividends.

H2: *Chinese firms reduced cash dividend payments before and after the split-share structure reform. The change in cash dividend payments is positively related to the change in the percentage ownership by the largest shareholder.*

5.3 Sample selection and data

5.3.1 Sample selection

To test my hypotheses, this chapter collected sample companies from non-financial firms listed on the Shanghai Stock Exchange and Shenzhen Stock Exchange. This chapter deleted firms that initiated the reform within one year after their initial public offerings because firms to which the state has large equity stakes tend to pay more dividends soon after new stock issues (Lee & Xiao, 2004). This chapter also excluded firms that committed to pay additional dividends after reform completion as compensation to PTS holders. Firms that report negative net income or net assets were also deleted because Chinese company law does not allow such companies to pay dividends. The reform initiation and completion years were different across companies. Throughout this chapter, I denote Year −1 as the year before the company initiated the split-share reform and Year 1 as the year after the firm completed the reform. If data was not available for Year −1 and Year 1, this chapter deleted those firms from the sample. As a result of the sample selection procedure, the final sample included 731 companies that completed the split-share structure reform process. All necessary data were obtained from the CCER database and each firm's annual reports.

5.3.2 Variables

This chapter focused on the change in cash dividend payments between Year −1 and post-reform years (Years 1, 2, and 3). Following Faccio et al. (2001) and La Porta et al. (2000b), this chapter adopted three variables to measure individual firm's cash dividend levels: cash dividends over earnings per share (*D_EPS*), cash dividends over stock price (*D_YIELD*), and cash dividends over sales per share (*D_SALE*) (see Table 5.1 for definition of variables). This chapter then computed changes in these variables before and after reform, which are respectively denoted by *CD_EPS*, *CD_YIELD*, and *CD_SALE*. For example, *CD_EPS* (−1, *t*) indicated the change in cash dividend per share between Year −1 and Year *t* (*t* = 1, 2, 3). For dividend measures, this chapter computed the industry-adjusted variable, which was computed by the firm's dividend variable minus the median of the dividend variable among same industry firms in order to control for industry characteristics (e.g., growth opportunities). This chapter also investigated the industry-adjusted dividend change (the change in the industry adjusted dividend variable before and after the reform) as well as the raw dividend change.

Table 5.1   Definition of variables

Variable	Definition
D_EPS	Cash dividends divided by earnings per share. We used earnings after tax and interest, but before extraordinary items.
D_YIELD	Cash dividends divided by stock price. The stock price was the year end price.
D_SALE	Cash dividends divided by net sales per share.
CD_EPS	Difference in D_EPS before and after the reform.
CD_YIELD	Difference in D_YIELD before and after the reform.
CD_SALE	Difference in D_SALE before and after the reform.
NPTSR	Proportion of non-publicly tradable shares over total outstanding shares.
LAR	Percentage ownership of the largest shareholder.
C_NPTSR	Change in NPTSR before and after the reform.
C_LAR	Change in LAR before and after the reform.
C_Earnings	Change in earnings (per share) before and after the reform.
SALESG	The percentage change in sales from the previous year. We computed this variable for the year before reform initiation.
ROE	Net income divided by net assets for the year before reform initiation.
DEBT	Total debts over total assets for the year before reform initiation.
SIZE	The logarithm of book value of total assets for the year before reform initiation.

The most important independent variables in this chapter were the changes in the proportion of NPTS over the total outstanding shares (C_NPTSR) and the percentage of ownership by the largest shareholder (C_LAR) before and after the reform. Previous studies found that the ratio of NPTS to total outstanding shares (NPTSR) is related to Chinese firms' dividend payments (Cheng et al., 2009; Huang et al., 2011; Wei & Xiao, 2009). As mentioned, typical Chinese firms have a single dominant shareholder whose ownership far exceeds that of the second largest shareholder (Chen et al., 2009; Cheng et al., 2009; Firth et al., 2006a; Gul et al.,

2010; Wang, 2005). This fact motivated this chapter to use the percentage of shares held by the largest shareholder (*LAR*) to measure the controlling shareholder's ownership. This chapter regressed the change in dividend payments (*CD_EPS*; *CD_YIELD*; *CD_SALE*) against the changes in the variables (*C_NPTSR*; *C_LAR*).

In addition to the above variables, the present analyses included several control variables. A change in cash dividend payments before and after the reform is likely to be associated with the change in firm performance during the period. Therefore, this chapter included the difference in earnings per share between Year −1 and post-reform years to control for performance effects (*C_Earnings*). Further, rich growth opportunities are likely to call for retained earnings to finance future investment projects (La Porta et al., 2000b; Faccio et al., 2001; Gul, 1999). Following La Porta et al. (2000b) and Faccio et al. (2001), this chapter controlled for investment opportunities by using the percentage of change in sales at Year −1 (*SALESG*). Lee and Xiao (2004) posited that *ROE* has a significant influence over cash dividend payments. As such, this chapter included *ROE* (net income divided by net assets) at Year −1 to control for the effect of absolute performance level on changes in cash dividends. Additionally, leverage potentially restricts cash dividend payments (Faccio et al., 2001; Huang et al., 2011; Kalay, 1982; Wei & Xiao, 2009). This chapter added the ratio of total debt over total assets at Year −1 (*DEBT*) to control for the effect of leverage. Faccio et al. (2001) and Fama and French (2001) documented that firm size has a positive impact on cash dividend payments; this chapter included the natural logarithm of total assets (*SIZE*) to control for the size effect.

5.3.3 Data description

Table 5.2 shows sample distribution by initiation and completion years of split-share structure reform. All sample firms began the reform in 2005 or 2006. Firms completed the reform in different years; most (76.9%) companies completed the reform in 2006.

Table 5.2 **Reform initiation and completion year distribution**

	Initiation year distribution		Completion year distribution	
	N	%	N	%
2005	238	32.56%	127	17.37%
2006	493	67.44%	562	76.88%
2007	0	0.00%	35	4.79%
2008	0	0.00%	7	0.96%
Total	731	100%	731	100%

This table indicates the distribution of reform initiation year and completion year. The sample consisted of 731 Chinese firms listed on the Shanghai Stock Exchange and Shenzhen Stock Exchange that conducted split-share structure reform.

Panel A of Table 5.3 exhibits means (medians) of absolute dividend level variables (*D_EPS*; *D_YIELD*; *D_SALE*) and ownership structure variables (*NPTSR* and *LAR*) by event year. Here, it is clearly shown that the dividend payments declined between Year −1 and Year 1. However, there were no continual downward trends between Year 1 and Year 3. This result was consistent with my hypothesis. In addition, *NPTSR* showed a continuous and sharp decline from 60.4% in Year −1 to 18.8% in Year 3. The finding suggests that the split-share structure reform substantially decreased the non-tradability of shares; during the post-reform period, the share non-tradability was not a striking feature of Chinese companies. Further, *LAR* experienced a decline before and after the reform (42.5% in Year −1 to 35.3% in Year 3). However, it would be noteworthy that controlling shareholders still held one-third of total outstanding shares. Concentrated ownership structure was a distinguishing feature of China listed companies even after the split-share structure reform.

Panel B of Table 5.3 presents the means (medians) of the dividend change variables (*CD_EPS*; *CD_YIELD*; *CD_SALE*; *C_NPTSR*; *C_LAR*). Consistent with my hypothesis, all the dividend change measures (*CD_EPS*; *CD_YIELD*; *CD_SALE*) showed negative values and most were significantly different from zero. As a result of the reform, C_NPTSR showed negative and significant values and the mean of C_NPTSR $(-1, 3)$ reached -41.6%, which suggests that the reform had a substantial impact on the Chinese segmented share structure. The mean and median of C_LAR were also negative and significant. However, C_LAR was small in absolute value compared to C_NPTSR. This difference allowed me to disentangle the effects of decreased NPTS on divided payments from the effect of reduced ownership concentration.

Finally, Panel C of Table 5.3 reports a summary of firm characteristics at Year -1. The mean annual sale growth was 29%, which suggests that sample companies had rich growth opportunities. High cash dividend payments were also likely to destroy minority shareholders' wealth.

Table 5.3   Descriptive statistics

Panel A indicates means (medians) of absolute cash dividend level variables (D_EPS; D_YIELD; D_SALE) and ownership structure variables ($NPTSR$; LAR) by event year. Year -1 refers to the year before the reform initiation. Year 1 refers to the year after the reform completion. Panel B shows means (medians) of the variables for raw cash dividend change (CD_EPS; CD_YIELD; CD_SALE) and variables for ownership structure change (CD_NPTSR; C_LAR). $(-1, t)$ denotes the time from year -1 to year t. Panel C presents descriptive statistics for other variables. Year -1 data is included in this panel. The entire sample consisted of 731 Chinese firms listed on the Shanghai Stock Exchange and Shenzhen Stock Exchange that conducted split-share structure reform. See Table 5.1 for definition of variables.

Panel A: Absolute dividend level and ownership structure variables

	Variables for absolute cash dividend level			Ownership structure variables	
	D_EPS	D_YIELD	D_SALE	NPTSR	LAR
Year −1	0.244(0.077)	0.011(0.004)	0.018(0.002)	0.604(0.621)	0.425(0.413)
Year 1	0.167(0)	0.004(0)	0.013(0)	0.428(0.432)	0.356(0.340)
Year 2	0.210(0.061)	0.006(0.002)	0.015(0.003)	0.379(0.376)	0.360(0.347)
Year 3	0.195(0.112)	0.006(0.003)	0.016(0.005)	0.188(0.094)	0.353(0.333)

Panel B: Changes in cash dividends and ownership structure variables

Interval	Variables for cash dividend change			Variables for ownership structure change	
	CD_EPS	CD_YIELD	CD_SALE	C_NPTSR	C_LAR
(−1, 1)	−0.077*** (−0.077)***	−0.007*** (−0.004)***	−0.005*** (−0.002)***	−0.176*** (−0.189)***	−0.0682*** (−0.073)***

Table5.3(continued)

(-1, 2)	-0.034 (-0.016)***	-0.005*** (-0.002)***	-0.003*** (0.001)***	-0.225*** (-0.245)***	-0.0644*** (-0.0658)***
(-1, 3)	-0.049*** (0.035)***	-0.005*** (-0.001)***	-0.002** (0.003)***	-0.416*** (-0.528)***	-0.0717*** (-0.0792)***

Panel C: Other variables

Variable (at year -1)	Mean	S.D.	Minimum	Median	Maximum
SALESG	0.293	1.225	-0.945	0.168	29.858
ROE	0.075	0.078	0.000	0.055	0.746
DEBT	0.503	0.175	0.013	0.514	1.421
Assets (billion RMB)	3.806	19.793	0.041	1.610	521

*** : Significant at the 1% level; ** : Significant at the 5% level; * : Significant at the 10% level

5.4 Empirical results

In the following section, I present the regression analyses in which the change in cash dividends is explained by C_NPTSR or C_LAR. To examine potential multicollinearity problems, this chapter presents a correlation matrix (see Table 5.4). The correlation coefficients of C_NPTSR and C_LAR were relatively high (0.26). However, other independent variables did not yield seriously high correlations except for SALESG and ROE (0.33).

Table 5.4 Correlation matrix

This table indicates correlation coefficients among variables that were used as dependent and independent variables in our most important regression analyses. For change variables, we used the change between Year -1 to Year 1. For other variables, Year -1 data was used. Year -1 refers to the year before the reform initiation. Year 1 refers to the year after the reform completion. The sample consisted of 731 Chinese firms listed on the Shanghai Stock Exchange and Shenzhen Stock Exchange that conducted split-share structure reform.

	CD_EPS (-1,1)	CD_YIELD (-1,1)	CD_SALE (-1,1)	C_NPTSR (-1,1)	C_LAR (-1,1)	C_Earnings (-1,1)	SALESG	ROE	DEBT	SIZE
CD_EPS(-1, 1)	1.00									
CD_YIELD(-1, 1)	0.52	1.00								

Table 5.4 (continued)

CD_SALE(-1, 1)	0.48	0.55	1.00						
C_NPTSR(-1, 1)	0.01	-0.08	0.00	1.00					
C_LAR(-1, 1)	0.04	0.03	0.06	0.26	1.00				
C_Earnings(-1, 1)	-0.08	-0.03	0.09	0.10	0.12	1.00			
SALESG	0.03	0.01	0.01	0.10	0.02	0.16	1.00		
ROE	-0.01	-0.26	-0.13	0.19	0.12	0.07	0.33	1.00	
DEBT	0.07	0.03	0.11	0.03	0.04	0.13	0.13	0.14	1.00
SIZE	-0.02	-0.22	-0.02	0.19	-0.04	0.10	0.03	0.22	0.21	1.00

Table 5.5 presents the regression results in which I used the change in raw (non-industry-adjusted) cash dividend variables as a dependent variable. In this table, I included C_NPTSR (Panel A) and C_LAR (Panel B) in the independent variable separately to avoid multicollinearity problems. All estimations include the reform initiation year dummy, which took a value of 1 for firms that initiated the reform in 2005 and 0 for those that initiated the reform in 2006. This was done to control for a potential relation between the early reform initiation and dividend payments; year and industry dummies were also included in the independent variable.①

Table 5.5 Regression results of the change in raw cash dividends

This table presents regression results of raw (non-industry-adjusted) cash dividend change variables (CD_EPS; CD_YIELD; CD_SALE). For all change variables (CD_EPS; CD_YIELD; CD_SALE; C_NPTSR; C_LAR; C_Earnings), the first three columns include the change between Year -1 and Year 1; the middle three columns include the change between Year -1 and Year 2; and the right three columns include the change between Year -1 and Year 3. Panel A (Panel B) adopted C_NPTSR (C_LAR) as the key independent variable. Year -1 data was used for other independent variables. The sample size decreased when we adopted longer intervals due to data availability. All models included an industry dummy, year dummy and reform initiation year dummy (1 for firms that initiated the reform in 2005 and 0 for those initiated in 2006); however, results are not reported. T-test statistics, computed by robust-standard errors, are reported in parentheses.

Interval (-1, t)	(-1, 1)			(-1, 2)			(-1, 3)		
Dependent variable	CD_EPS (-1,t)	CD_YIELD (-1,t)	CD_SALE (-1,t)	CD_EPS (-1,t)	CD_YIELD (-1,t)	CD_SALE (-1,t)	CD_EPS (-1,t)	CD_YIELD (-1,t)	CD_SALE (-1,t)

---

① We used CSRC industry classification code and employed the 1-digit industry classification code for non-manufacturing firms. We specified the industry of manufacturing companies according to the 2-digit industry classification code.

Table5.5(continued)

Panel A: Results when using C_NPTSR as an independent variable

Constant	0.18 (0.68)	0.06*** (5.12)	-0.01 (-0.39)	-0.09 (-0.19)	0.07*** (4.84)	0.04 (1.50)	0.61** (2.00)	0.07*** (5.03)	0.06** (2.15)
C_NPTSR (-1, t)	0.14 (1.12)	0.00 (0.06)	0.01 (0.61)	0.28 (1.13)	0.00 (0.73)	0.01 (1.56)	0.04 (0.45)	0.00 (0.15)	0.01 (1.61)
C_Earnings (-1, t)	-0.11*** (-2.69)	0.00 (0.21)	0.01* (1.77)	-0.20*** (-3.06)	0.01*** (3.64)	0.01*** (2.74)	-0.14*** (-3.70)	0.00* (1.96)	0.00 (0.34)
SALESG	0.01 (1.40)	0.00** (2.30)	0.00 (1.11)	0.01 (0.92)	0.00 (1.45)	0.00 (0.05)	0.00 (0.86)	0.00** (2.44)	0.00 (1.22)
ROE	-0.12 (-0.50)	-0.06*** (-6.76)	-0.07*** (-3.54)	-0.19 (-0.50)	-0.03*** (-3.02)	-0.04* (-1.90)	-0.01 (-0.06)	-0.05*** (-4.66)	-0.07** (-2.52)
DEBT	0.25** (2.36)	0.01*** (3.58)*	0.02** (2.33)	0.13 (0.92)	0.01*** (3.74)	0.03** (2.37)	0.10 (1.04)	0.01*** (2.80)	0.03*** (2.88)
SIZE	-0.02 (-1.35)	-0.00*** (-5.29)	-0.00 (-0.84)	-0.00 (-0.15)	-0.00*** (-5.56)	-0.00** (-2.42)	-0.04*** (-2.61)	-0.00*** (-5.12)	-0.00*** (-3.17)
N	731	731	731	658	658	658	637	637	636
R-squared	0.018	0.157	0.082	0.024	0.179	0.091	0.028	0.132	0.127

Panel B: Results when using C_LAR as an independent variable

Constant	0.08 (0.30)	0.06*** (4.94)	-0.01 (-0.62)	-0.40 (-0.68)	0.07*** (4.62)	0.03 (1.01)	0.58* (1.88)	0.07*** (5.08)	0.05* (1.91)
C_LAR (-1, t)	0.20 (1.55)	0.01* (1.72)	0.02** (1.98)	0.38* (1.89)	0.01 (1.16)	0.02 (1.48)	0.27** (2.06)	0.01** (2.16)	0.04*** (2.59)
C_Earnings (-1, t)	-0.11*** (-2.76)	0.00 (0.07)	0.01 (1.64)	-0.20*** (-3.22)	0.01*** (3.56)	0.01*** (2.70)	-0.14*** (-3.83)	0.00* (1.88)	0.00 (0.26)
SALESG	0.01 (1.60)	0.00** (2.39)	0.00 (1.29)	0.01 (1.18)	0.00 (1.51)	0.00 (0.20)	0.00 (0.96)	0.00** (2.49)	0.00 (1.37)
ROE	-0.14 (-0.58)	-0.06*** (-6.96)	-0.07*** (-3.62)	-0.22 (-0.59)	-0.04*** (-3.00)	-0.04* (-1.88)	-0.06 (-0.27)	-0.05*** (-4.68)	-0.08*** (-2.65)
DEBT	0.24** (2.29)	0.01*** (3.58)	0.02** (2.31)	0.11 (0.73)	0.01*** (3.69)	0.03** (2.31)	0.10 (1.04)	0.01*** (2.79)	0.03*** (2.88)
SIZE	-0.01 (-0.98)	-0.00*** (-5.04)	-0.00 (-0.57)	0.01 (0.35)	-0.00*** (-5.21)	-0.00** (-1.98)	-0.04** (-2.47)	-0.00*** (-5.07)	-0.00*** (-2.92)
Industry dummy	Yes								
N	731	731	731	658	658	658	637	637	636
R-squared	0.019	0.159	0.086	0.024	0.180	0.091	0.033	0.136	0.136

***: Significant at the 1% level; **: Significant at the 5% level; *: Significant at the 10% level

Panel A of Table 5.5 shows that C_NPTSR had an insignificant coefficient in all estimations. This result suggests that the decrease in NPTS was not a driving force for the reduced dividend payments after the reform. In contrast, Panel B of Table 5.5 shows that *C_LAR* had a positive coefficient in all models; some were statistically significant. Of note, all models that used the dividend change between Year −1 and Year 3 engendered a positive and significant coefficient on *C_LAR*.

Table 5.6 presents the regression results with the change in industry-adjusted dividend variable as a dependent variable. In this table, I did not include industry dummy variables. Again, Panel A shows that *C_NPTSR* did not have a significant coefficient (at the 5% level) in all models. In contrast, all models included in Panel B engendered a positive coefficient on *C_LAR*; the coefficient was significant at the 1% level when we adopted the dividend change between Year −1 to Year 3. Given that it may take a few years for firms to adjust their dividend policy in response to the ownership structure change, we should place more stress on the regression results for longer intervals. This chapter argues that the reduction in cash dividends before and after the reform is attributable to the decline in the percentage of ownership of controlling shareholders, rather than to the reduction in NPTS.

Table 5.6 Regression results of the change in industry-adjusted cash dividends

This table presents regression results of industry-adjusted cash dividend change variables (*CD_EPS*; *CD_YIELD*; *CD_SALE*). For all change variables (*CD_EPS*; *CD_YIELD*; *CD_SALE*; *C_NPTSR*; *C_LAR*; *C_Earnings*), the first three columns include the change between Year −1 and Year 1; the middle three columns include the change between Year −1 and Year 2; and the right three columns include the change between Year −1 and Year 3. Panel A (Panel B) adopted *C_NPTSR* (*C_LAR*) as the key independent variable. Year −1 data was used for other independent variables. The sample size decreased when we adopted longer intervals due to data availability. All models included an industry dummy, year dummy and reform initiation year dummy (1 for firms that initiated the reform in 2005 and 0 for those initiated in 2006); however, results are not reported. T-test statistics, computed by robust-standard errors, are reported in parentheses.

Interval (−1, t)	(−1, 1)			(−1, 2)			(−1, 3)		
Dependent variable	CD_EPS (−1, t)	CD_YIELD (−1, t)	CD_SALE (−1, t)	CD_EPS (−1, t)	CD_YIELD (−1, t)	CD_SALE (−1, t)	CD_EPS (−1, t)	CD_YIELD (−1, t)	CD_SALE (−1, t)
Panel A: Results when using *C_NPTSR* as an independent variable									
Constant	0.24 (0.87)	0.06*** (4.74)	0.01 (0.35)	−0.04 (−0.09)	0.07*** (4.75)	0.04 (1.48)	0.68** (2.13)	0.06*** (4.37)	0.07*** (2.67)
C_NPTSR (−1, t)	0.10 (0.74)	−0.00 (−0.23)	0.01 (0.84)	0.27 (1.11)	0.00 (0.77)	0.01 (1.51)	0.07 (0.79)	0.00 (0.65)	0.01* (1.94)

Table 5.6 (continued)

C_Earnings (-1, t)	-0.12*** (-3.04)	-0.00 (-0.03)	0.01 (1.45)	-0.23*** (-3.29)	0.01*** (3.22)	0.01** (2.37)	-0.16*** (-4.20)	0.00 (1.53)	0.00 (0.02)
SALESG	0.01* (1.96)	0.00*** (3.02)	0.00 (1.23)	0.01* (1.81)	0.00** (2.10)	0.00 (0.44)	0.01 (0.98)	0.00*** (2.67)	0.00 (1.20)
ROE	-0.15 (-0.60)	-0.06*** (-6.43)	-0.06*** (-3.32)	-0.31 (-0.82)	-0.04*** (-3.25)	-0.05** (-2.30)	-0.08 (-0.33)	-0.05*** (-4.67)	-0.08*** (-2.82)
DEBT	0.24** (2.27)	0.01*** (3.00)	0.02** (2.26)	0.09 (0.63)	0.01*** (2.95)	0.03** (2.32)	0.11 (1.14)	0.01* (1.84)	0.03*** (2.96)
SIZE	-0.02 (-1.25)	-0.00*** (-4.78)	-0.00 (-0.88)	0.00 (0.08)	-0.00*** (-5.18)	-0.00* (-1.92)	-0.04** (-2.37)	-0.00*** (-4.35)	-0.00*** (-3.18)
N	731	731	731	658	658	658	637	637	636
R-squared	0.017	0.128	0.047	0.015	0.128	0.055	0.024	0.109	0.081

Panel B: Results when using C_LAR as an independent variable

Constant	0.17 (0.60)	0.06*** (4.72)	0.00 (0.08)	-0.36 (-0.62)	0.06*** (4.47)	0.02 (0.98)	0.64** (1.98)	0.06*** (4.39)	0.06** (2.33)
C_LAR (-1, t)	0.24* (1.83)*	0.01** (1.99)	0.02* (1.96)	0.46** (2.39)	0.01** (2.05)	0.02* (1.72)	0.35*** (2.67)	0.01*** (2.96)	0.04*** (2.81)
C_Earnings (-1, t)	-0.13*** (-3.18)	-0.00 (-0.20)	0.01 (1.31)	-0.24*** (-3.53)	0.01*** (3.06)	0.01** (2.30)	-0.16*** (-4.36)	0.00 (1.43)	-0.00 (-0.08)
SALESG	0.01** (2.14)	0.00*** (3.14)	0.00 (1.43)	0.01** (2.08)	0.00** (2.22)	0.00 (0.63)	0.01 (1.17)	0.00*** (2.84)	0.00 (1.44)
ROE	-0.18 (-0.77)	-0.06*** (-6.72)	-0.07*** (-3.40)	-0.36 (-0.97)	-0.04*** (-3.28)	-0.05** (-2.30)	-0.14 (-0.60)	-0.05*** (-4.75)	-0.08*** (-3.00)
DEBT	0.23** (2.21)	0.01*** (2.98)	0.02** (2.23)	0.06 (0.40)	0.01*** (2.81)	0.02** (2.21)	0.11 (1.13)	0.01* (1.82)	0.03*** (2.95)
SIZE	-0.01 (-0.94)	-0.00*** (-4.62)	-0.00 (-0.56)	0.02 (057)	-0.00*** (-4.76)	-0.00 (-1.44)	-0.03** (-2.20)	-0.00*** (-4.28)	-0.00*** (-2.86)
N	731	731	731	658	658	658	637	637	636
R-squared	0.020	0.131	0.051	0.017	0.132	0.056	0.031	0.117	0.091

***: Significant at the 1% level; **: Significant at the 5% level; *: Significant at the 10% level

Table 5.7 presents the regression results when I included both C_NPTS and C_LAR. Again, C_LAR had a positive and significant coefficient when I adopted the dividend change during Year -1 and Year 3 as a dependent variable. In contrast, C_NPTSR was insignificant in all models. Overall, the regression results indicate no significant relationship between the changes in cash dividends and NPTS. This result does not support previous studies' arguments that Chinese controlling shareholders prefer cash dividends because of the non-tradability of their shares (Cheng et al., 2009; Huang et al., 2011; Wei & Xiao, 2009). In other words, controlling shareholders prefer cash dividends regardless of non-tradability of their shares. It is difficult for controlling shareholders to sell their shares and realize capital gains for the following reasons: ① controlling shareholders desire to keep their voting power and ② stock prices will show serious fluctuations if controlling shareholders sell their stocks. As such, this chapter argues that the inherent illiquidity of shares makes controlling shareholders prefer cash dividends. Regarding control variables, firm size and performance (*ROE*) are positively related to the cash dividend change; leverage is negatively related.

Table 5.7 Regression results of the change in cash dividends

This table presents regression results of cash dividend change variables (*CD_EPS*; *CD_YIELD*; *CD_SALE*). For all change variables (*CD_EPS*; *CD_YIELD*; *CD_SALE*; *C_NPTSR*; *C_LAR*; *C_Earnings*), the first three columns include the change between Year −1 and year 1; the middle three columns include the change between Year −1 and Year 2; and the right three columns include the change between Year −1 and Year 3. Panel A (Panel B) adopted change in raw cash dividends (change in industry-adjusted cash dividends) as the dependent variable. *C_NPTSR* and *C_LAR* are the key independent variables. Year −1 data was used for other independent variables. The sample size decreased when we adopted longer intervals due to data availability. All models included an industry dummy, year dummy and reform initiation year dummy (1 for firms that initiated the reform in 2005 and 0 for those initiated in 2006); however, results are not reported. *T*-test statistics, computed by robust-standard errors, are reported in parentheses.

Interval (−1, *t*)	(−1, 1)			(−1, 2)			(−1, 3)		
Dependent variable	CD_EPS (−1, *t*)	CD_YIELD (−1, *t*)	CD_SALE (−1, *t*)	CD_EPS (−1, *t*)	CD_YIELD (−1, *t*)	CD_SALE (−1, *t*)	CD_EPS (−1, *t*)	CD_YIELD (−1, *t*)	CD_SALE (−1, *t*)
Panel A: Results of the change in raw (non-industry-adjusted) cash dividends									
Constant	0.15 (0.55)	0.06*** (4.95)	−0.01 (−0.59)	−0.20 (−0.43)	0.07*** (4.62)	0.04 (1.31)	0.58* (1.92)	0.07*** (4.98)	0.06** (2.00)
C_LAR (−1, *t*)	0.16 (1.16)	0.01* (1.68)	0.02* (1.86)	0.29 (1.59)	0.00 (0.93)	0.01 (1.11)	0.27* (1.79)	0.01** (2.10)	0.03** (2.30)
C_NPTSR (−1, *t*)	0.10 (0.76)	−0.00 (−0.28)	0.00 (0.06)	0.20 (0.82)	0.00 (0.43)	0.01 (1.26)	−0.00 (−0.05)	−0.00 (−0.42)	0.01 (0.81)
C_Earnings (−1, *t*)	−0.11*** (−2.77)	0.00 (0.09)	0.01 (1.63)	−0.21*** (−3.17)	0.01*** (3.53)	0.01*** (2.62)	−0.14*** (−3.83)	0.00* (1.88)	0.00 (0.22)
SALESG	0.01 (1.52)	0.00** (2.42)	0.00 (1.26)	0.01 (0.99)	0.00 (1.47)	0.00 (0.09)	0.00 (1.00)	0.00** (2.51)	0.00 (1.29)

Table5. 7(continued)

ROE	-0.15 (-0.63)	-0.06** (-6.89)	-0.07*** (-3.65)	-0.24 (-0.61)	-0.04*** (-3.02)	-0.04* (-1.93)	-0.06 (-0.28)	-0.05*** (-4.67)	-0.08*** (-2.62)
DEBT	0.25** (2.35)	0.01*** (3.56)	0.02** (2.31)	0.12 (0.88)	0.01*** (3.71)	0.03** (2.34)	0.10 (1.03)	0.01*** (2.79)	0.03*** (2.89)
SIZE	-0.02 (-1.19)	-0.00*** (-5.09)	-0.00 (-0.57)	0.00 (0.12)	-0.00*** (-5.27)	-0.00** (-2.17)	-0.04** (-2.51)	-0.00*** (-5.04)	-0.00*** (-2.96)
N	731	731	731	658	658	658	637	637	636
R-squared	0.020	0.160	0.086	0.026	0.180	0.093	0.033	0.137	0.137
Panel B: Results of the change in industry-adjusted cash dividends									
Constant	0.20 (0.70)	0.06*** (4.55)	0.00 (0.15)	-0.19 (-0.40)	0.06*** (4.43)	0.03 (1.24)	0.65** (2.05)	0.06*** (4.33)	0.07** (2.51)
C_LAR (-1, t)	0.23 (1.55)	0.01** (2.03)	0.02* (1.80)	0.38** (2.14)	0.01* (1.81)	0.02 (1.38)	0.35** (2.22)	0.01*** (2.67)	0.04** (2.48)
C_NPTSR (-1, t)	0.04 (0.32)	-0.00 (-0.62)	0.00 (0.28)	0.18 (0.71)	0.00 (0.21)	0.01 (1.10)	0.01 (0.12)	-0.00 (-0.16)	0.01 (1.06)
C_Earnings (-1, t)	-0.13*** (-3.17)	-0.00 (-0.17)	0.01 (1.31)	-0.24*** (-3.46)	0.01*** (3.05)	0.01** (2.23)	-0.16*** (-4.37)	0.00 (1.42)	-0.00 (-0.12)
SALESG	0.01** (2.16)	0.00*** (3.27)	0.00 (1.39)	0.01** (1.97)	0.00** (2.19)	0.00 (0.51)	0.01 (1.19)	0.00*** (2.84)	0.00 (1.35)
ROE	-0.19 (-0.77)	-0.06*** (-6.62)	-0.07*** (-3.44)	-0.37 (-0.97)	-0.04*** (-3.29)	-0.05** (-2.34)	-0.14 (-0.60)	-0.05*** (-4.73)	-0.08*** (-2.96)
DEBT	0.23** (2.24)	0.01*** (2.95)	0.02** (2.22)	0.07 (0.54)	0.01*** (2.84)	0.03** (2.25)	0.11 (1.12)	0.01* (1.82)	0.03*** (2.95)
SIZE	-0.01 (-1.04)	-0.00*** (-4.54)	-0.00 (-0.60)	0.01 (0.42)	-0.00*** (-4.78)	-0.00 (-1.62)	-0.03** (-2.25)	-0.00*** (-4.26)	-0.00*** (-2.94)
N	731	731	731	658	658	658	637	637	636
R-squared	0.020	0.132	0.052	0.017	0.132	0.058	0.031	0.117	0.093

*** : Significant at the 1% level; ** : Significant at the 5% level; * : Significant at the 10% level

5.5 Absolute levels of cash dividends, NPTS, and ownership concentration

To further test whether the inherent illiquidity of shares, rather than the non-tradability of shares, was associated with controlling shareholders' preferences for cash dividends, this chapter conducted cross-sectional regressions of the absolute level of dividend payments (D_EPS ; D_YIELD ; D_SALE) during the post-reform period. This analysis used all available data from the sample companies after the reform completion (until the year 2009). For example, four years' data (2006 to 2009) were included for firms that completed the reform in 2005. If the inherent illiquidity of shares engendered the determinant of preference for cash dividends, controlling shareholders that had a high percentage of ownership would have forced firms to pay higher dividends even after the reform, which substantially decreased NPTS.

This chapter conducts Tobit regressions to examine this idea. The most important independent variables were LAR and $NPTSR$. I used the same control variables as in the former analyses [$C\_Earnings$ was replaced by earnings per share (Earnings)]; however, the reform initiation year dummy was deleted in this analysis. The results are presented in Table 5.8. The coefficient of LAR was positive and highly significant for all estimations (Panel B). This result was consistent with the view that controlling shareholders, who own a substantial portion of shares, prefer cash dividends even after the substantial reduction in NPTS. Importantly, Panel A engenders insignificant coefficients on $NPTSR$; the controlling shareholders' preference for cash dividends was attributable to the inherent illiquidity of their shares rather than to share non-tradability. With respect to control variables, I found that more profitable firms were more likely to pay higher cash dividends and firms with rich investment opportunities were more likely to pay fewer cash dividends. Further, leverage was negatively related to cash dividend payments and firm size was positively associated with the level of cash dividends. These results are consistent with findings of previous studies (Faccio et al., 2001; Fama & French, 2001; Gul, 1999; Huang et al., 2011; Kalay, 1982; La Porta et al., 2000b; Wei & Xiao, 2009).

Table 5.8   **Tobit regression results**

This table presents the Tobit regression results of the absolute cash dividend levels (*D_EPS*; *D_YIELD*; *D_SALE*). All available data for sample firms after the split-share reform completion are included in this analysis. For example, data from 2006 to 2009 are included for companies that completed the reform in 2005. Panel A (Panel B) adopted *NPTSR* (*LAR*) as a key independent variable. All models include year and industry dummy variables; however, results are not reported. *T*-test statistics are in parentheses.

Dependent variable	D_EPS	D_YIELD	D_SALE
Panel A: Results when using NPTSR as an independent variable			
Constant	−2.89*** (−8.54)	−0.07*** (−12.29)	−0.21*** (−10.63)
NPTSR	0.06 (0.71)	0.00 (0.28)	0.01 (1.15)
Earnings	0.10** (2.29)	0.01*** (9.25)	0.02*** (9.58)
SALESG	−0.02 (−1.36)	−0.00* (−1.90)	−0.00** (−2.32)
ROE	−0.21 (−1.15)	0.00 (0.92)	0.01* (1.90)
DEBT	−0.71*** (−7.61)	−0.02*** (−9.95)	−0.08*** (−14.56)
SIZE	0.17*** (10.35)	0.00*** (14.32)	0.01*** (12.45)
Year dummy	\multicolumn{3}{c}{Yes}		
Industry dummy	Yes		
N	2730	2730	2729
Panel B: Results when using LAR as an independent variable			
Constant	−2.79*** (−8.22)	−0.07*** (−11.92)	−0.21*** (−10.31)
LAR	0.28*** (2.80)	0.01*** (3.53)	0.02** (2.57)
Earnings	0.10** (2.28)	0.01 (9.25)	0.02*** (9.58)
SALESG	−0.02 (−1.44)	−0.00** (−2.15)	−0.00** (−2.43)
ROE	−0.22 (−1.16)	0.00 (0.89)	0.01* (1.93)
DEBT	−0.70*** (−7.51)	−0.02*** (−9.82)	−0.08*** (−14.49)
SIZE	0.16*** (9.64)	0.00*** (13.38)	0.01*** (11.78)
Year dummy	Yes		
Industry dummy	Yes		
N	2730	2730	2729

***: Significant at the 1% level; **: Significant at the 5% level; *: Significant at the 10% level

5.6 Conclusion

This chapter attempted to reveal factors that influence Chinese controlling shareholders' preferences for cash dividends. Specifically, this chapter investigated the relation between the changes in cash dividends, proportion of NPTS, and percentage of ownership of controlling shareholders before and after the split-share structure reform. The split-share structure reform was an exogenous shock for firms that substantially decreased NPTS and ownership concentration. Compared to the reduction in NPTS, ownership concentration showed a relatively small decline. Therefore, this chapter took advantage of this research opportunity to discriminate the effects of share non-tradability on cash dividend payments from the effect of ownership concentration. Further, I stress that the reform provided me with data that was less subject to endogeneity problems.

In sum, this chapter found a significant reduction in cash dividend payments before and after the reform. However, the reduction in NPTS was not significantly related to the decline in cash dividends. Rather, the decline in the percentage of ownership of the controlling shareholder was significantly associated with the reduction in cash dividends. Therefore, this chapter argues that share non-tradability, *per se*, does not cause controlling shareholders' preferences for cash dividends, rather, it should be attributable to the inherent illiquidity of their shares. The additional analysis indicated that the percentage of ownership of the controlling shareholder was positively associated with the absolute level of cash dividends during the post-reform period. In contrast, the proportion of NPTS over the total outstanding shares was not significantly related to the absolute cash dividend level. This result reinforced my argument.

My analyses make an important contribution to the literature. Previous studies have argued that non-tradability of shares, held by controlling shareholders, is an important factor that is associated with Chinese corporate cash dividend policy (Cheng et al., 2009; Huang et al., 2011; Wei & Xiao, 2009). However, my results provide clear evidence that non-tradability of shares is not the main driver of Chinese controlling shareholders' preferences for cash dividends. This chapter interprets this contradiction as, before the split-share structure reform, there was an automatic correlation between the proportion of NPTS and the percentage of ownership of controlling shareholders. As a result, the former had a positive correlation with cash dividend payments. This chapter also contributes to the literature in presenting additional evidence of the common view that concentrated ownership structures cause expropriation of minority shareholders by controlling shareholders (Claessens et al., 2000; Dyck & Zingales, 2004; La Porta et al., 2000b).

6. Conclusion and implications

This book examines empirically the effectiveness of corporate governance mechanisms in China and explores whether corporate governance mechanisms provide adequate protection for minority shareholders in China. More specifically, it explores ① the influence of corporate governance mechanisms on firm stock performance during the global financial crisis; ② long-term stock performance following top executive turnover; ③ the linkage between cash dividend payment and ownership structure.

In Chapter 3, this book explores the relationship between corporate governance mechanisms on firm stock performance during the global financial crisis. This chapter finds that Chinese state-owned enterprises (SOEs) that performed poorly before the global financial crisis performed better during the crisis, especially when they relied on bank debt. The result suggests that state ownership mitigates financial constraints during times of financial crisis. Large shareholders' ownership has a U-shaped relation to crisis-period performance, which suggests ownership concentration mitigates financial constraints and engenders expropriation problems. This chapter also finds that managerial ownership is positively associated with crisis-period performance of SOEs. This result suggests that managerial ownership mitigates expropriation problems in SOEs. Finally, Chinese firms that employed a reputable accounting auditor experienced a small reduction in firm value during the global financial crisis.

In Chapter 4, this book examines the impact of Chief Executive Officer (CEO) turnover on subsequent stock performance for a sample of 666

China's listed firms for the period 2001-2007. This chapter documents that CEO turnover before split-share reform resulted in no improvement in stock performance; after split-share reform, however, there is a significant improvement in stock performance following CEO turnover in firms that had exhibited negative shareholder return, but not for firms that exhibited non-negative return. The post-reform result suggests that controlling shareholders have an incentive to discipline their CEOs based on financial performance when firms have exhibited negative shareholder return after split-share reform.

Chapter 5 investigates the relation between changes in cash dividend payments, non-public tradable shares, and the percentage of ownership of the controlling shareholder in Chinese firms before and after the split-share structure reform. This chapter finds a significant reduction in cash dividends before and after the reform. Importantly, the reduction in cash dividends was significantly related to the reduction in the largest shareholder's ownership; however, it was not associated with the decline in non-publicly tradable shares. These results suggest that Chinese controlling shareholders' preferences for cash dividends is attributable to the inherent illiquidity of their shares rather than non-tradability of shares.

The presented results should help researchers and/or practitioners better understand Chinese corporate governance and the protection of minority shareholder's wealth in China's listed firms. Specifically, the studies here suggest that an incentive of controlling shareholders is important in China within its context of low legal protection for minority shareholders and large ownership concentration: state ownership had a positive impact on firm value during the global financial crisis (Chapter 3); post-CEO turnover performance improves only when shareholder return is negative and CEOs face great pressure from minority shareholders to improve stock performance during the post-reform period (Chapter 4). In normal situations, state ownership is an ineffective corporate governance mechanism. However, during the financial crisis, as state controlling shareholders had an incentive to prop up SOEs, SOEs outperformed non-SOEs (Chapter 3). Additionally, split-share structure reform, to a certain extent, aligns the interests of controlling and minority shareholder in terms of capital gain, and improves corporate governance in China's listed firms: shares owned by controlling shareholders become tradable, and the degree of controlling shareholders' preference for cash dividends declines due to the decrease of ownership concentration (Chapter 4); post-CEO turnover performance improves when shareholder return is negative (Chapter 5). However, as long as controlling shareholders have an incentive to keep enough equity to achieve their own goals by avoiding trading of shares on stock exchanges, the conflict of interests between controlling-minority shareholders associated with stock performance, will not be eliminated. During the post-reform period, controlling shareholders still prefer cash dividends due to their incentive to maintain control of listed firms (Chapter 5), and stock performance following CEO turnover does not improve when shareholder return is non-negative and controlling shareholders have an incentive to pursue non performance-related objectives (e.g., social and political objectives) (Chapter 4).

References

[1] AGUILERA RV, A CUERVO-CAZURRA. 2004. Codes of good governance worldwide: what is the trigger? [J]. Organization Studies, 25(3): 415-443.

[2] AHN S, W CHOI. 2009. The role of bank monitoring in corporate governance: evidence from borrowers' earnings management behavior[J]. Journal of Banking & Finance, 33(2): 425-434.

[3] ALCHIAN AA, H DEMSETZ. 1972. Production, information costs, and economic organization[J]. The American Economic Review, 62(5): 777-795.

[4] ALISON G, D MAYES. 1991. Technical inefficiency in manufacturing industries[J]. The Economic Journal, 101(406): 523-538.

[5] ALLEN F, J QIAN, M QIAN. 2005. Law, finance, and economic growth in China[J]. Journal of Financial Economics, 77(1): 57-116.

[6] BAEK JS, JK KANG, KS PARK. 2004. Corporate governance and firm value: evidence from the Korean financial crisis[J]. Journal of Financial Economics, 71(2): 265-313.

[7] BAEK JS, JK KANG, I LEE. 2006. Business groups and tunneling: evidence from private securities offerings by Korean chaebols[J]. The Journal of Finance, 61(5): 2415-2449.

[8] BAI CE, DD LI, Z TAO, Y WANG. 2000. A multitask theory of state enterprise reform[J]. Journal of Comparative Economics, 28(4): 716-738.

[9] BAI CE, J LU, Z TAO. 2006. The multitask theory of state en-

terprise reform: empirical evidence from China[J]. The American Economic Review, 96(2): 353-357.

[10] BAI CE, J LU, Z TAO. 2009. How does privatization work in China? [J]. Journal of Comparative Economics, 37(3): 453-470.

[11] BAI CE, Q LIU, J LU, FM SONG, J ZHANG. 2004. Corporate governance and market valuation in China[J]. Journal of Comparative Economics, 32(4): 599-616.

[12] BALVERS R, YR WU, E GILLILAND. 2000. Mean reversion across national stock markets and parametric contrarian investment strategies[J]. The Journal of Finance, 55(2):745-772.

[13] BARBER BM, JD LYON. 1997. Detecting long-run abnormal stock returns: the empirical power and specification of test statistics[J]. Journal of Financial Economics, 43(3): 341-372.

[14] BARRO JR, R BARRO. 1990. Pay, performance, and turnover of bank CEOs[J]. Journal of Labor Economics, 8(4): 448-481.

[15] BEASLEY MS. 1996. An empirical analysis of the relation between the board of director composition and financial statement fraud[J]. The Accounting Review, 71(4): 443-465.

[16] BENNEDSEN M, HC KONGSTED, KM NIELSEN. 2008. The causal effect of board size in the performance of small and medium-sized firms[J]. Journal of Banking & Finance, 32(6): 1098-1109.

[17] BERGER AN, I HASAN, M ZHOU. 2009. Bank ownership and efficiency in China: what will happen in the world's largest nation? [J]. Journal of Banking & Finance, 33(1): 113-130.

[18] BERGER PG, E OFEK. 1995. Diversification's effect on firm value[J]. Journal of Financial Economics, 37(1): 39-65.

[19] BERKMAN H, RA COLE, LJ FU. 2009. Expropriation through loan guarantees to related parties: evidence from China[J]. Journal of Banking & Finance, 33(1): 141-156.

[20] BERLE AA, GC MEANS. 1969. The modern corporation and private property[J]. Economic Journal, 20(6): 25-49.

[21] BHAGAT S, B BOLTON. 2008. Corporate governance and firm performance[J]. Journal of Corporate Finance, 14(3): 257-273.

[22] BOONE AL, LC FIELD, JM KARPOFF, CG RAHEJA. 2007. The determinants of corporate board size and composition: an empirical analysis[J]. Journal of Financial Economics, 85(1): 66-101.

[23] BOROKHOVICH KA, R PARRINO, T TRAPANI. 1996. Outside directors and CEO selection[J]. Journal of Financial and Quantitative Analysis, 31(3): 337-355.

[24] BORTOLOTTI B, A BELTRATTI. The nontradable share reform in the Chinese stock market [R]. http://ssrn.com/abstract = 944412, 2006-11-15.

[25] BUSHMAN RM, AJ SMITH. 2001. Financial accounting information and corporate governance[J]. Journal of Accounting and Economics, 32(1-3): 237-333.

[26] BYERS SS, LP FIELDS, DR FRASER. 2008. Are corporate governance and bank monitoring substitutes: evidence from the perceived value of bank loans[J]. Journal of Corporate Finance, 14(4): 475-483.

[27] BYRD J, K HICKMAN. 1992. Do outside directors monitor managers? evidence from tender offer bids[J]. Journal of Financial Economics, 32(2): 195-221.

[28] CAMPBELL JY, RL SHILLER. 1988. Stock prices, earnings, and expected dividends[J]. The Journal of Finance, 43(3): 661-676.

[29] CAMPELLO M, JR GRAHAM, CR HARVEY. 2010. The real effects of financial constraints: evidence from a financial crisis[J]. Journal of Financial Economics, 97(3): 470-487.

[30] CARHART MM. 1997. On persistence in mutual fund performance[J]. The Journal of Finance, 52(1): 57-82.

[31] CHAN K, J WANG, KCJ WEI. 2004. Underpricing and long-term performance of IPOs in China[J]. Journal of Corporate Finance, 10(3): 409-430.

[32] Chang EC, SML Wong. Chief Executive Officer Turnovers and

the Performance of China's Listed Enterprises[R]. http://ssrn.com/abstract = 644741, 2005-01-09.

[33] CHANG EC, SML WONG. 2009. Governance with multiple objectives: evidence from top executive turnover in China[J]. Journal of Corporate Finance, 15(2): 230-244.

[34] Chen DH, JPH Fan, TJ Wong. Politically connected CEOs, corporate governance and post-IPO performance of China's partially privatized firms[R]. http://ssrn.com/abstract = 642441, 2005-01-03.

[35] CHEN D, JPH FAN, TJ WONG. Decentralization and the structure of Chinese corporate boards: do politicians jeopardize professionalism? [A]. In TSUI YBAS, L CHEUNG(eds.). China's domestic private firms: multi-disciplinary perspectives on management and performance[C]. New York: ME Sharpe, 2006:147-170.

[36] CHEN G, M FIRTH, L XU. 2009. Does the type of ownership control matter? evidence from China's listed companies[J]. Journal of Banking & Finance, 33(1): 171-181.

[37] CHEN Z. 2003. Capital markets and legal development: the China case[J]. China Economic Review, 14(4): 451-472.

[38] CHENG LTW, HG FUNG, TY LEUNG. 2009. Dividend preference of tradable-share and non-tradable-shareholders in mainland China [J]. Accounting & Finance, 49(2): 291-316.

[39] CHI J, Q SUN, M YOUNG. 2011. Performance and characteristics of acquiring firms in the Chinese stock markets[J]. Emerging Markets Review, 12(2): 152-170.

[40] CHI W, Y WANG. 2009. Ownership, performance and executive turnover in China[J]. Journal of Asian Economics, 20(4): 465-478.

[41] CLAESSENS S, S DJANKOV, LHP LANG. 2000. The separation of ownership and control in east Asian corporations[J]. Journal of Financial Economics, 58(1-2): 81-112.

[42] CLAESSENS S, S DJANKOV, JPH FAN, LHP LANG. 2002. Disentangling the incentive and entrenchment effects of large shareholdings

[J]. The Journal of Finance, 57(6): 2741-2771.

[43] CLARKE DC. 2003. Corporate governance in China: an overview[J]. China Economic Review, 14(4): 494-507.

[44] COLES JL, ND DANIEL, L NAVEEN. 2008. Boards: does one size fit all? [J]. Journal of Financial Economics, 87(2): 329-356.

[45] CONYON MJ, L HE. 2011. Executive compensation and corporate governance in China[J]. Journal of Corporate Finance, 17(4): 1158-1175.

[46] COOPER M. 2008. New thinking in financial market regulation: dismantling the 「split share structure」 of Chinese listed companies[J]. Journal of Chinese Political Science, 13(1): 53-78.

[47] COUGHLAN AT, RM SCHMIDT. 1985. Executive compensation, management turnover, and firm performance: an empirical investigation[J]. Journal of Accounting and Economics, 7(1-3): 43-66.

[48] CRONQVIST H, M NILSSON. 2003. Agency costs of controlling minority shareholders[J]. Journal of Financial and Quantitative Analysis, 38(4): 695-719.

[49] CSRC. Guidelines for introducing independent directors to the board of directors of listed companies[EB/OL]. (關於在上市公司建立獨立董事制度的指導意見) http://www.csrc.gov.cn, 2001-08-16. (in Chinese)

[50] CSRC. (2005) A notice on issues relating to the reform of ownership rights segregation[EB/OL]. (關於股權分置改革問題的通知) http://www.csrc.gov.cn, 2005-04-29. (in Chinese)

[51] CUÑAT V, M GUADALUPE. 2005. How does product market competition shape incentive contracts? [J]. Journal of the European Economic Association, 3(5): 1058-1082.

[52] DAHYA J, JJ MCCONNELL. 2005. Outside directors and corporate board decisions[J]. Journal of Corporate Finance, 11(1-2): 37-60.

[53] DAHYA J, O DIMITROV, JJ MCCONNELL .2008. Dominant

shareholders, corporate boards and corporate value: a cross-country analysis[J]. Journal of Financial Economics, 87(1): 73-100.

[54] DECHOW PM, RG SLOAN, AP SWEENEY. 1996. Causes and consequences of earnings manipulations: an analysis of firms subject to enforcement actions by the SEC[J]. Contemporary Accounting Research, 13(1): 1-36.

[55] DEFOND ML, CW PARK. 1999. The effect of competition on CEO turnover[J]. Journal of Accounting and Economics, 27(1): 35-56.

[56] DEFOND ML, M HUNG. 2004. Investor protection and corporate governance: evidence from worldwide CEO turnover[J]. Journal of Accounting Research, 42(2): 269-312.

[57] DEMB A, FF NEUBAUER. 1992. The corporate board: confronting the paradoxes [J]. Long Range Planning, 25(3): 9-20.

[58] DENG X, Z WANG. 2006. Ownership structure and financial distress: evidence from public-listed companies in China[J]. International Journal of Management, 23(3): 486-502.

[59] DENIS DJ, DK DENIS. 1995. Performance changes following top management dismissals[J]. The Journal of Finance, 50(4): 1029-1057.

[60] DENIS DJ, DK DENIS, A SARIN. 1997a. Ownership structure and top executive turnover[J]. Journal of Financial Economics, 45(2): 193-221.

[61] DENIS DJ, DK DENIS, A SARIN. 1997b. Agency problems, equity ownership and corporate diversification[J]. The Journal of Finance, 52(1): 135-160.

[62] DENIS DK. 2001. Twenty-five years of corporate governance research …and counting[J]. Review of Financial Economics, 10(3): 191-212.

[63] DENIS DK, JJ MCCONNELL. 2003. International corporate governance[J]. Journal of Financial and Quantitative Analysis, 38(1): 1-36.

[64] DEWENTER KL, PH MALATESTA. 2001. State-owned and privately owned firms: an empirical analysis of profitability, leverage, and labor intensity[J]. The American Economic Review, 91(1): 320-334.

[65] DHARWADKAR R, G GEORGE, P BRANDES. 2000. Privatization in emerging economies: an agency theory prospective[J]. Academy of Management Review, 25(3): 650-669.

[66] DIAMOND DW. 1984. Financial intermediation and delegated monitoring[J]. The Review of Economic Studies, 51(3): 393-414.

[67] DIAMOND D, R VERROCCHIO. 1991. Disclosure, liquidity and the cost of capital[J]. The Journal of Finance, 46(4): 1325-1355.

[68] DIN IS. 2005. Politicians and banks: political influences on government-owned banks in emerging markets[J]. Journal of Financial Economics, 77(2): 453-479.

[69] DITTMAR A, J MAHRT-SMITH, H SERVAES. 2003. International corporate governance and corporate cash holdings[J]. Journal of Financial and Quantitative Analysis, 38(1): 111-133.

[70] DIXIT A. 1997. Power of incentives in private versus public organizations[J]. The American Economic Review, 87(2): 378-382.

[71] DONALDSON L, JH DAVIS. 1991. Stewardship theory or agency theory: CEO governance and shareholder returns[J]. Australian Journal of Management, 16(1): 49-64.

[72] DURNEV ART, EH KIM. 2005. To steal or not to steal: firm attributes, legal environment, and valuation[J]. The Journal of Finance, 60(3): 1461-1493.

[73] DYCK A, L ZINGALES. 2004. Private benefits of control: an international comparison[J]. The Journal of Finance, 59(2): 537-599.

[74] DYE RA. 1993. Auditing standards, legal liability and auditor wealth[J]. Journal of Political Economy, 101(5): 887-914.

[75] EASTERBROOK FH. 1984. Two agency-cost explanations of dividends[J]. The American Economic Review, 74(4): 650-659.

[76] EICHHOLTZ P, N KOK. 2008. How does the market for corpo-

rate control function for property companies? [J]. Journal of Real Estate Finance and Economics, 36(2): 141-163.

[77] EISENBERG T, S SUNDGREN, MT WELLS. 1998. Larger board size and decreasing firm value in small firms[J]. Journal of Financial Economics, 48(1): 35-54.

[78] FACCIO M, LHP LANG. 2002. The ultimate ownership of western European corporations[J]. Journal of Financial Economics, 65(3): 365-395.

[79] FACCIO M, LHP LANG, L YOUNG. 2001. Dividends and expropriation[J]. The American Economic Review, 91(1): 54-78.

[80] FAMA EF. 1980. Agency problems and the theory of the firm [J]. Journal of Political Economy, 88(2): 288-307.

[81] FAMA EF. 1985. What's different about banks? [J]. Journal of Monetary Economics, 15(1): 29-39.

[82] FAMA EF, KR FRENCH. 1988. Permanent and temporary components of stock prices[J]. Journal of Political Economy, 96(2): 246-273.

[83] FAMA EF, KR FRENCH .1992. The cross-section of expected stock returns[J]. The Journal of Finance, 47(2): 427-465.

[84] FAMA EF, KR FRENCH. 1993. Common risk factors in the returns on stocks and bonds[J]. Journal of Financial Economics, 33(1): 3-56.

[85] FAMA EF, KR FRENCH. 1996. Multifactor explanations of asset pricing anomalies[J]. The Journal of Finance, 51(1): 55-84.

[86] FAMA EF, KR FRENCH. 2001. Disappearing dividends: changing firm characteristics or lower propensity to pay[J]. Journal of Financial Economics, 60(1): 3-43.

[87] FAMA EF, MC JENSEN. 1983a. Separation of ownership and control[J]. Journal of Law and Economics, 26(2): 301-325.

[88] FAMA EF, MC JENSEN. 1983b. Agency problems and residuals claims[J]. Journal of Law and Economics, 26(2): 327-349.

[89] FAN DKK, CM LAU, M YOUNG. 2007. Is China's corporate governance beginning to come of age? the case of CEO turnover[J]. Pacific-Basin Finance Journal, 15(2): 105-120.

[90] FAN JPH, TJ WONG. 2002. Corporate ownership structure and the informativeness of accounting earnings in east Asia [J]. Journal of Accounting and Economics, 33(3): 401-425.

[91] FAZZARI SM, RG HUBBARD, BC PETERSEN, AS BLINDER, JM POTERBA. 1988. Financing constraints and corporate investment [J]. Brookings Papers on Economic Activity, 1988 (1): 141-206.

[92] FINKELSTEIN S, RAD'AVENI. 1994. CEO duality as a double-edged sword: how boards of directors balance entrenchment avoidance and unity of command[J]. Academy of Management Journal, 37(5): 1079-1108.

[93] FIRTH M, C LIN, SML WONG. 2008. Leverage and investment under a state-owned bank lending environment: evidence from China[J]. Journal of Corporate Finance, 14(5): 642-653.

[94] FIRTH M, PMY FUNG, OM RUI. 2006a. Corporate performance and CEO compensation in China[J]. Journal of Corporate Finance, 12(4): 693-714.

[95] FIRTH M, PMY FUNG, OM RUI. 2006b. Firm performance, governance structure, and top management turnover in a transitional economy[J]. Journal of Management Studies, 43(6): 1289-1330.

[96] FIRTH M, PMY FUNG, OM RUI. 2007. How ownership and corporate governance influence chief executive pay in China's listed firms [J]. Journal of Business Research, 60(7): 776-785.

[97] FREDRICKSON JW, DC HAMBRICK, S BAUMRIN. 1988. A model of CEO dismissal[J]. Academy of Management Review, 13(2): 255-270.

[98] GAO L, G KLING. 2008. Corporate governance and tunneling: empirical evidence from China [J]. Pacific-Basin Finance Journal, 16(5): 591-605.

[99] GIBELMAN M, SR GELMAN. 2002. On the departure of a chief executive officer: scenarios and implications[J]. Administration in Social Work, 26: 63-82.

[100] GILLAN SL. 2006. Recent developments in corporate governance: an overview[J]. Journal of Corporate Finance, 12(3): 381-402.

[101] GLADSTEIN DL. 1984. Groups in context: a model of task group effectiveness[J]. Administrative Science Quarterly, 29(4): 499-517.

[102] GLEASON KC, LK MATHUR, I MATHUR. 2000. The interrelationship between culture, capital structure, and performance: evidence from European retailers[J]. Journal of Business Research, 50(2): 185-191.

[103] GLOSTEN LR, PR MILGROM. 1985. Bid, ask and transaction prices in a specialist market with heterogeneously informed traders[J]. Journal of Financial Economics, 14(1): 71-100.

[104] GOMEZ-MEJIA LR, H TOSI, T HINKIN. 1987. Managerial control, performance, and executive compensation[J]. The Academy of Management Journal, 30(1): 51-70.

[105] GOMPERS P, J ISHII, A METRICK. 2003. Corporate governance and equity prices[J]. The Quarterly Journal of Economics, 118(1): 107-155.

[106] GORDON RH, W LI. 2003. Government as a discriminating monopolist in the financial market: the case of China[J]. Journal of Public Economics, 87(2): 283-312.

[107] GORTON G, FA SCHMID. 2000. Universal banking and the performance of German firms[J]. Journal of Financial Economics, 58(1-2): 29-80.

[108] GUEST PM. 2008. The determinants of board size and composition: evidence from the UK[J]. Journal of Corporate Finance, 14(1): 51-72.

[109] GUGLER K, BB YURTOGLU. 2003. Corporate governance

and dividend pay-out policy in Germany[J]. European Economic Review, 47(4): 731-758.

[110] GUL FA. 1999. Government share ownership, investment opportunity set and corporate policy choices in China[J]. Pacific-Basin Finance Journal, 7(2): 157-172.

[111] GUL FA, JB KIM, AA QIN. 2010. Ownership concentration, foreign shareholding, audit quality, and stock price synchronicity: evidence from China[J]. Journal of Financial Economics, 95(3): 425-442.

[112] GUNASEKARAGE A, K HESS, AJ HU. 2007. The influence of the degree of state ownership and the ownership concentration on the performance of listed Chinese companies[J]. Research in International Business and Finance, 21(3): 379-395.

[113] HART OD. 1983. The market mechanism as an incentive scheme[J]. Bell Journal of Economics, 14(2): 366-382.

[114] HASKEL J. 1991. Imperfect competition, work practices and productivity growth[J]. Oxford Bulletin of Economics and Statistics, 53(3): 265-279.

[115] HAY DA, GS LIU. 1997. The efficiency of firms: what difference does competition make? [J]. The Economic Journal, 107(442): 597-617.

[116] HEALY PM, KG PALEPU. 2001. Information asymmetry, corporate disclosure, and the capital markets: a review of the empirical disclosure literature[J]. Journal of Accounting and Economics, 31(1-3): 405-440.

[117] HECKMAN JJ. 1979. Sample selection bias as a specification error[J]. Econometrica, 47(1): 153-161.

[118] HERMALIN BE. 1994. Heterogeneity in organizational form: why otherwise identical firms choose different incentives for their managers [J]. RAND Journal of Economics, 25(4): 518-537.

[119] HERMALIN BE, MS WEISBACH. 2003. Boards of directors as endogenously determined institutions: a survey of the economic literature

[J]. Economic Policy Review, 9(1): 7-26.

[120] HILLIER D, P MCCOLGAN. 2009. Firm performance and managerial succession in family managed firms[J]. Journal of Business Finance & Accounting, 36(3-4): 461-484.

[121] HIMMELBERG CP, RG HUBBARD, D PALIA. 1999. Understanding the determinants of managerial ownership and the link between ownership and performance[J]. Journal of Financial Economics, 53(3): 353-384.

[122] HOLMSTROM B. 1982. Moral hazard in teams[J]. Bell Journal of Economics, 13(2): 324-340.

[123] HOPE O-K, WB THOMAS. 2008. Managerial empire building and firm disclosure[J]. Journal of Accounting Research, 46(3): 591-626.

[124] HOPT KJ, H KANDA, MJ ROE, E WYMEERSCH, S PRIGGE (eds.). Comparative corporate governance[C]. Oxford: Clarendon Press. 1998.

[125] HOSHI T, A KASHYAP, D SCHARFSTEIN. 1991. Corporate structure, liquidity, and investment: evidence from Japanese industrial groups[J]. The Quarterly Journal of Economics, 106(1): 33-60.

[126] HOSKISSON RE, L EDEN, C LAU, M WRIGHT. 2000. Strategy in emerging economies[J]. Academy of Management Journal, 43(3): 249-267.

[127] HU Y, X ZHOU. 2008. The performance effect of managerial ownership: evidence from China[J]. Journal of Banking & Finance, 32(10): 2099-2110.

[128] HUANG G, F SONG. 2005. The financial and operating performance of China's newly listed H-firms[J]. Pacific-Basin Finance Journal, 13(1): 53-80.

[129] HUANG JJ, Y SHEN, Q SUN. 2011. Nonnegotiable shares, controlling shareholders, and dividend payments in China[J]. Journal of Corporate Finance, 17(1): 122-133.

[130] HUSON MR, PH MALATESTA, R PARRINO. 2004. Managerial succession and firm performance[J]. Journal of Financial Economics, 74(2): 237-275.

[131] HUSON MR, R PARRINO, LT STARKS. 2001. Internal monitoring mechanisms and CEO turnover: a long-term perspective[J]. The Journal of Finance, 56(6): 2265-2297.

[132] IVASHINA V, D SCHARFSTEIN. 2010. Bank lending during the financial crisis of 2008[J]. Journal of Financial Economics, 97(3): 319-338.

[133] JAMES C. 1987. Some evidence on the uniqueness of bank loans[J]. Journal of Financial Economics, 19(2): 217-235.

[134] JANUSZEWSKI SI, J KOKE, JK WINTER. 2002. Product market competition, corporate governance and firm performance: an empirical analysis for Germany[J]. Research in Economics, 56(3): 299-332.

[135] JEGADEESH N, S TITMAN. 1993. Returns to buying winners and selling losers: implications for stock market efficiency[J]. The Journal of Finance, 48(1): 65-91.

[136] JENSEN MC. 1986. Agency costs of free cash flow, corporate finance, and takeovers[J]. The American Economic Review, 76(2): 323-329.

[137] JENSEN MC. 1989. Eclipse of the public corporation[J]. Harvard Business Review, September/October 67(5): 61-74.

[138] JENSEN MC. 1993. The modern industrial revolution, exit, and the failure of internal control systems[J]. The Journal of Finance, 48(3): 831-880.

[139] JENSEN MC, KJ MURPHY. 1990. Performance pay and top-management incentives[J]. Journal of Political Economy, 98(2): 225-264.

[140] JENSEN MC, RS RUBACK. 1983. The market for corporate control: the scientific evidence[J]. Journal of Financial Economics, 11(1-4): 5-50.

[141] JENSEN MC, WH MECKLING. 1976. Theory of the firm: managerial behavior, agency costs and ownership structure[J]. Journal of Financial Economics, 3(4): 305-360.

[142] JENTER D, K LEWELLEN. Performance-induced CEO turnover[R]. http://areas.kenan-flagler.unc.edu/finance/JHFinance/Documents, 2010-01-22.

[143] JIANG G, CMC LEE, H YUE. 2010. Tunneling through intercorporate loans: the China experience[J]. Journal of Financial Economics, 98(1): 1-20.

[144] JOHNSON S, P BOONE, A BREACH, E FRIEDMAN. 2000. Corporate governance in the Asian financial crisis[J]. Journal of Financial Economics, 58(1-2): 141-186.

[145] KALAY A. 1982. Stockholder-bondholder conflict and dividend constraints[J]. Journal of Financial Economics, 10(2): 211-233.

[146] KANG J-K, A SHIVDASANI. 1995. Firm performance, corporate governance, and top executive turnover in Japan[J]. Journal of Financial Economics, 38(1): 29-58.

[147] KANG J-K, A SHIVDASANI, T YAMADA. 2000. The effect of bank relations on investment decisions: an investigation of Japanese takeover bids[J]. The Journal of Finance, 55(5): 2197-2218.

[148] KANG J-K, RM STULZ. 2000. Do banking shocks affect borrowing firm performance? an analysis of the Japanese experience[J]. The Journal of Business, 73(1): 1-23.

[149] KAPLAN SN. 1994. Top executives, turnover, and firm performance in Germany[J]. Journal of Law, Economics and Organization, 10(1): 142-159.

[150] KAPLAN SN, BA MINTON. 1994. Appointments of outsiders to Japanese boards: determinants and implications for managers[J]. Journal of Financial Economics, 36(2): 225-258.

[151] KATO T, C LONG. 2006a. CEO turnover, firm performance, and enterprise reform in China: evidence from micro data[J]. Journal of

Comparative Economics, 34(4): 796-817.

[152] KATO T, C LONG. 2006b. Executive turnover and firm performance in China[J]. The American Economic Review, 96(2): 363-367.

[153] KHORANA A. 2001. Performance changes following top management turnover: evidence from open-end mutual funds[J]. Journal of Financial and Quantitative Analysis, 36(3): 371-393.

[154] KHWAJA AI, A MIAN. 2005. Do lenders favor politically connected firms? rent provision in an emerging financial market[J]. The Quarterly Journal of Economics, 120(4): 1371-1411.

[155] KLAPPER LF, I LOVE. 2004. Corporate governance, investor protection, and performance in emerging markets[J]. Journal of Corporate Finance, 10(5): 703-728.

[156] KORNAI J. 1979. Resource-constrained versus demand-constrained systems [J]. Econometrica, 47(4): 801-819.

[157] KUPPUSWAMY V, B VILLALONGA. Does diversification create value in the presence of external financing constraints? evidence from the 2007-2009 financial crisis[R]. http://ssrn.com/abstract=1571255, 2010-12-02.

[158] LA PORTA R, F LOPEZ-DE-SILANES, A SHLEIFER. 1999. Corporate ownership around the world[J]. The Journal of Finance, 54(2): 471-518.

[159] LA PORTA R, F LOPEZ-DE-SILANES, A SHLEIFER, R VISHNY. 1997. Legal determinants of external finance[J]. The Journal of Finance, 52(3): 1131-1150.

[160] LA PORTA R, F LOPEZ-DE-SILANES, A SHLEIFER, R VISHNY. 1998. Law and finance[J]. Journal of Political Economy, 106(6): 1113-1155.

[161] LA PORTA R, F LOPEZ-DE-SILANES, A SHLEIFER, R VISHNY. 2000a. Investor protection and corporate governance[J]. Journal of Financial Economics, 58(1-2): 3-27.

[162] LA PORTA R, F LOPEZ-DE-SILANES, A SHLEIFER, R VISHNY. 2000b. Agency problems and dividend policies around the world[J]. The Journal of Finance, 55(1): 1-33.

[163] LA PORTA R, F LOPEZ-DE-SILANES, A SHLEIFER, R VISHNY. 2002. Investor Protection and corporate valuation[J]. The Journal of Finance, 57(3):1147-1170.

[164] LANG LHP, RM STULZ. 1992. Contagion and competitive intra-industry effects of bankruptcy announcements: an empirical analysis [J]. Journal of Financial Economics, 32(1): 45-60.

[165] LANG LHP, RM STULZ. 1994. Tobin's Q, corporate diversification and firm performance[J]. Journal of Political Economy, 102(6): 1248-1280.

[166] LEE CJ, X XIAO. Tunneling dividends[R]. http://www.baf.cuhk.edu.hk/ research/cig/pdf_download/LeeXiao.pdf, 2004-12-02.

[167] LEMMON ML, KV LINS. 2003. Ownership structure, corporate governance, and firm value: evidence from the east Asian financial crisis[J]. The Journal of Finance, 58(4): 1445-1468.

[168] LEUZ C, KV LINS, FE WARNOCK. 2009. Do Foreigners invest less in poorly governed firms? [J]. Review of Financial Studies, 22(8): 3245-3285.

[169] LI D, F MOSHIRIAN, P NGUYEN, LW TAN. 2007. Managerial ownership and firm performance: evidence from China's privatizations [J]. Research in International Business and Finance, 21(3): 396-413.

[170] LI G. 2010. The pervasiveness and severity of tunneling by controlling shareholders in China[J]. China Economic Review, 21(2): 310-323.

[171] LI K, H YUE, L ZHAO. 2009. Ownership, institutions and capital structure: evidence from China[J]. Journal of Comparative Economics, 37(3): 471-490.

[172] LI K, T WANG, Y-L CHEUNG, P JIANG. Privatization with negotiation: evidence from the split share structure reform in China[R].

http://www. rotman. utoronto. ca/userfiles/departments/finance/File/Li, Kai_Privatization%20with%20Negotiation_28Sept07.pdf, 2007-03-02.

[173] LI K, T WANG, Y-L CHEUNG, P JIANG. 2011. Privatization and risk sharing: evidence from the split share structure reform in China[J]. Review of Financial Studies, 24(7): 2499-2525.

[174] LI W. 1997. The impact of economic reform on the performance of Chinese state enterprises, 1980-1989[J]. Journal of Political Economy, 105(5): 1080-1106.

[175] LI ZQ, ZW WANG, Z SUN. 2004. Tunneling and ownership structure of a firm: evidence from controlling shareholder's embezzlement of listed company's funds in China[J]. Accounting Research, 25/12: 3-13.

[176] LIAO G, X CHEN, X JING, J SUN. 2009. Policy burdens, firm performance, and management turnover[J]. China Economic Review, 20(1): 15-28.

[177] LIAO J, Q SUN, M YOUNG. The advisory role of the board: evidence from the implementation of independent director system in China [R]. http://ssrn.com/abstract=1361202, 2009-03-17.

[178] LICHT AN, C GOLDSCHMIDT, SH SCHWARTZ. 2005. Culture, law, and corporate governance[J]. International Review of Law and Economics, 25(2): 229-255.

[179] LIN C, Y MA, DW SU. 2009. Corporate governance and firm efficiency: evidence from China's publicly listed firms[J]. Managerial and Decision Economics, 30(3): 193-209.

[180] LIN X, Y ZHANG, N ZHU. 2009. Does bank ownership increase firm value? evidence from China[J]. Journal of International Money and Finance, 28(4): 720-737.

[181] LIN Y-H, J-R CHIOU, Y-R CHEN. 2010. Ownership structure and dividend preference: evidence from China's privatized state-owned enterprises[J]. Emerging Markets Finance and Trade, 46(1): 56-74.

[182] LIN ZJ. 2005. New rules on protecting public shareholders in the Chinese stock market[J]. The Company Lawyer, 26(7): 222-224.

[183] LIPTON M, JW LORSCH. 1992. A modest proposal for improved corporate governance[J]. Business Lawyer, 48(1): 59-77.

[184] LIU C, J LIU, K UCHIDA. Do independent boards effectively monitor management? evidence from Japan during the financial crisis[A]. In: SUN W, J STEWART, D POLLARD (eds.). Corporate governance and the global financial crisis: international perspectives[C]. Cambridge University Press. 2011: 188-214.

[185] LIU Q. 2006. Corporate governance in China: current practices, economic effects and institutional determinants[J]. CESifo Economic Studies, 52(2): 415-453.

[186] LIU Q, Z LU. 2007. Corporate Governance and earnings management in the Chinese listed companies: a tunneling perspective[J]. Journal of Corporate Finance, 13(5): 881-906.

[187] LIU X, S WHITE. 2001. Comparing innovation systems: a framework and application to China' transitional context[J]. Research Policy, 30(7): 1091-1114.

[188] LOUGHRAN T, JR RITTER. 1995. The new issues puzzle[J]. The Journal of Finance, 50(1): 23-51.

[189] LU D, S THANGAVELU, Q HU. 2005. Biased lending and non-performing loans in China's banking sector[J]. Journal of Development Studies, 41(6): 1071-1091.

[190] LUMMER SL, JJ MCCONNELL. 1989. Further evidence on the bank lending process and the capital-market response to bank loan agreements[J]. Journal of Financial Economics, 25(1): 99-122.

[191] LV C, X ZHOU. 2005. Corporate governance and payout incentive-based on agency cost and tunneling[J]. NanKai Business Review, 8: 9-17 (in Chinese).

[192] LYON JD, BM BARBER, C-L TSAI. 1999. Improved methods for tests of long-run abnormal stock returns[J]. The Journal of Finance, 54(1): 165-201.

[193] MALLETTE P, KL FOWLER. 1992. Effects of board composi-

tion and stock ownership on the adoption of poison pills[J]. Academy of Management Journal, 35(5): 1010-1035.

[194] MANNE HG. 1965. Mergers and the market for corporate control[J]. Journal of Political Economy, 73(2): 110-120.

[195] MARRIS R. 1963. A model of the 「managerial」 enterprise [J]. The Quarterly Journal of Economics, 77(2): 185-209.

[196] MARTIN KJ, JJ MCCONNELL. 1991. Corporate performance, corporate takeovers, and management turnover[J]. The Journal of Finance, 46(2): 671-687.

[197] MAURY B, A PAJUSTE. 2002. Controlling shareholders, agency problems and dividend policy in Finland [J]. Liketaloudellinen Aikakauskirja (The Finish Journal of Business Economics), 2002(1):15-45.

[198] MCCONNELL JJ, H SERVAES. 1990. Additional evidence on equity ownership and corporate value[J]. Journal of Financial Economics, 27(2): 595-612.

[199] MCCONNELL JJ, H SERVAES. 1995. Equity ownership and the two faces of debt[J]. Journal of Financial Economics, 39(1): 131-157.

[200] MCNEIL C, G NIEHAUS, E POWERS. 2004. Management turnover in subsidiaries of conglomerates versus stand-alone firms[J]. Journal of Financial Economics, 72(1): 63-96.

[201] MEEK GK, CB ROBERT, SJ GRAY. 1995. Factors influencing voluntary annual report disclosures by U.S., U.K. and continental Europe multinational corporations[J]. Journal of International Business Studies, 26(3): 555-572.

[202] MICHAELY R, WH SHAW. 1995. Does the choice of auditor convey quality in an initial public offering? [J]. Financial Management, 24(4): 15-30.

[203] MITTON T. 2002. A cross-firm analysis of the impact of corporate governance on the east Asian financial crisis[J]. Journal of Finan-

cial Economics, 64(2): 215-241.

[204] MOERLAND PW. 1995. Corporate ownership and control structures: an international comparison[J]. Review of Industrial Organization, 10(4): 443-464.

[205] MORCK R, A SHLEIFER, RW VISHNY. 1988. Management ownership and market valuation: an empirical analysis[J]. Journal of Financial Economics, 20(1-3): 293-315.

[206] MORCK R, D STRANGELAND, BY YEUNG. Corporate control and economic growth: the Canadian disease? [R]. http://ssrn.com/abstract=141192, 1998-12-26.

[207] MORCK R, D WOLFENZON, B YEUNG. 2005. Corporate governance, economic entrenchment, and growth[J]. Journal of Economic Literature, 43(3): 655-720.

[208] MYERS SC. 1977. Determinants of corporate borrowing[J]. Journal of Financial Economics, 5(2): 147-175.

[209] NALEBUFF BJ, JE STIGLITZ. 1983. Prizes and incentives: towards a general theory of compensation and competition[J]. Bell Journal of Economics, 14(1): 21-43.

[210] NICKELL SJ. 1996. Competition and corporate performance [J]. Journal of Political Economy, 104(4): 724-746.

[211] NOGATA D, K UCHIDA, H MORIYASU. Corporate governance and stock price performance during the financial crisis: evidence from Japan[R]. http://ssrn.com/abstract=1501723, 2010-10-30.

[212] NOLAN P. 1996. Large firms and industrial reform in former planned economics: the case of China[J]. Cambridge Journal of Economics, 20(1): 1-29.

[213] OPLER CT, S TITMAN. 1994. Financial distress and corporate performance[J]. The Journal of Finance 49(3): 1015-1040.

[214] PARK A, L BRANDT, J GILES. 2003. Competition under credit rationing: theory and evidence from rural China[J]. Journal of Development Economics, 71(2): 463-495.

[215] PENG MW, SJ ZHANG, XC LI. 2007. CEO duality and firm performance during China's institutional transition[J]. Management and Organization Review, 3(2): 205-225.

[216] POTERBA JM, LH SUMMERS. 1988. Mean reversion in stock prices: evidence and implications[J]. Journal of Financial Economics, 22(1): 27-59.

[217] QI D, W WU, H ZHANG. 2000. Shareholding structure and corporate performance of partially privatized firms: evidence from listed Chinese companies[J]. Pacific-Basin Finance Journal, 8(5): 587-610.

[218] QIANG Q. 2003. Corporate governance and state-owned shares in China listed companies[J]. Journal of Asian Economics, 14(5): 771-783.

[219] QIU HY, SH YAO. 2009. Share merger reform, corporate governance and firm value in China [R]. http://ssrn.com/abstract = 1275699, 2008-10-01.

[220] RAHMAN M. 1998. The role of accounting in the east Asian financial crisis: lessons learned? [J]. Transnational Corporations, 7(3): 1-51.

[221] RAJAN RG, L ZINGALES. 1998. Which capitalism? lessons from the east Asian crisis[J]. Journal of Applied Corporate Finance, 11(3): 40-48.

[222] RECHNER PL, DR DALTON. 1991. CEO duality and organizational performance: a longitudinal analysis [J]. Strategic Management Journal, 12(2): 155-160.

[223] RITTER JR. 1991. The long-run performance of initial public offerings[J]. The Journal of Finance, 46(1): 3-27.

[224] ROSE NL, A SHEPARD. Firm diversification and CEO compensation: managerial ability or executive entrenchment? [R]. http://www.nber.org/papers/ w4723, 1994-04-01.

[225] ROSENSTEIN S, JG WYATT. 1990. Outside directors, board independence, and shareholder wealth[J]. Journal of Financial Economics, 26(2): 175-191.

[226] SANTOS JAC, AS RUMBLE. 2006. The American keiretsu and universal banks: investing, voting and sitting on nonfinancials' corporate boards[J]. Journal of Financial Economics, 80(2): 419-454.

[227] SAPIENZA P. 2004. The effects of government ownership on bank lending[J]. Journal of Financial Economics, 72(2): 357-384.

[228] SCHARFSTEIN D. 1988. The disciplinary role of takeovers[J]. The Review of Economic Studies, 55(2): 185-199.

[229] SHAO L, CC KWOK, O GUEDHAMI. 2010. National culture and dividend policy[J]. Journal of International Business Studies, 41(8): 1391-1414.

[230] SHAW ME. Group dynamics: the psychology of small group behavior[M]. New York: McGraw-Hill, 1981.

[231] SHEARD P. 1989. The main bank system and corporate monitoring and control in Japan[J]. Journal of Economic Behavior & Organization, 11(3): 399-422.

[232] SHEN W, AA CANNELLA. 2002. Power dynamics within top management and their impacts on CEO dismissal followed by inside succession[J]. Academy of Management Journal, 45(6): 1195-1208.

[233] SHEN W, C LIN. 2009. Firm profitability, state ownership, and top management turnover at the listed firms in China: a behavioral perspective[J]. Corporate Governance: An International Review, 17(4): 443-456.

[234] SHLEIFER A, RW VISHNY. 1994. Politicians and firms[J]. The Quarterly Journal of Economics, 109(4): 995-1025.

[235] SHLEIFER A, RW VISHNY. 1997. A survey of corporate governance[J]. The Journal of Finance, 52(2): 737-783.

[236] SHORT H, K KEASEY. 1999. Managerial ownership and the performance of firms: evidence from the UK[J]. Journal of Corporate Finance, 5(1): 79-101.

[237] SMITH CW, JB WARNER. 1979. On financial contracting: an analysis of bond covenants[J]. Journal of Financial Economics, 7(2): 117

-161.

[238] SUN Q, WHS TONG. 2003. China share issue privatization: the extent of its success[J]. Journal of Financial Economics, 70(2): 183-222.

[239] TANG QQ, DL LUO. 2006. The tunneling of cash dividends and the dividend of controlling shareholders[J]. Finance and Trade Research, 1: 92-97 (in Chinese).

[240] TIAN JJ, C-M LAU. 2001. Board composition, leadership structure and performance in Chinese shareholding companies[J]. Asia Pacific Journal of Management, 18(2): 245-263.

[241] TIAN L, S ESTRIN. 2007. Debt financing, soft budget constraints, and government ownership: evidence from China[J]. Economics of Transition, 15(3): 461-481.

[242] VAN DEN BERGHE LAA, A LEVRAU. 2004. Evaluating boards of directors: what constitutes a good corporate board? [J]. Corporate Governance: An International Review, 12(4): 461-478.

[243] WANG C. 2005. Ownership and operating performance of Chinese IPOs[J]. Journal of Banking & Finance, 29(7): 1835-1856.

[244] WANG JW. 2010. A comparison of shareholder identity and governance mechanisms in the monitoring of CEOs of listed companies in China[J]. China Economic Review, 21(1): 24-37.

[245] WARNER JB, RL WATTS, KH WRUCK. 1988. Stock prices and top management changes[J]. Journal of Financial Economics, 20(1-3): 461-492.

[246] WEI G, JZ XIAO. 2009. Equity ownership segregation, shareholder preferences, and dividend policy in China[J]. The British Accounting Review, 41(3): 169-183.

[247] WEI Z, F XIE, S ZHANG. 2005. Ownership structure and firm value in China's privatized firms: 1991-2001[J]. Journal of Financial and Quantitative Analysis, 40(1): 87-108.

[248] WEISBACH MS. 1988. Outside directors and CEO turnover

[J]. Journal of Financial Economics, 20(1-3): 431-460.

[249] WHITED TW. 1992. Debt, liquidity constraints and corporate investment: evidence from panel data[J]. The Journal of Finance, 47(4): 1425-1459.

[250] XU X, Y WANG. 1999. Ownership structure and corporate governance in Chinese stock companies[J]. China Economic Review, 10(1): 75-98.

[251] YEH Y-H, P-G SHU, T-S LEE, Y-H SU. 2009. Non-tradable share reform and corporate governance in the Chinese stock market[J]. Corporate Governance: An International Review, 17(4): 457-475.

[252] YERMACK D. 1996. Higher market valuation of companies with a small board of directors[J]. Journal of Financial Economics, 40(2): 185-211.

[253] YERMACK D. 2006. Board members and company value[J]. Financial Markets and Portfolio Management, 20(1): 33-47.

[254] YI Y, D KE, X ZHANG. 2007. Shareholder wealth effect of dividend policy: empirical evidence from the Chinese securities market[J]. Frontiers of Business Research in China, 1(3): 437-455.

[255] YUAN HQ. 2001. Analysis on the dividend policy of listed companies in China[J]. The Study of Finance and Economics, 27: 33-41 (in Chinese).

[256] ZHANG A, Y ZHANG, R ZHAO. 2001. Impact of ownership and competition on the productivity of Chinese enterprises[J]. Journal of Comparative Economics, 29(2): 327-346.

[257] ZHOU X, C LV. 2008. Does high dividend payout protect investors? a case study of chihong zinc & germanium[J]. Frontiers of Business Research in China, 2008(3): 417-439.

[258] ZOU H, S WONG, C SHUM, J XIONG, J YAN. 2008. Controlling-minority shareholder incentive conflicts and directors' and officers' liability insurance: evidence from China[J]. Journal of Banking & Finance, 32(12): 2636-2645.

Appendix

Appendix 1

According to a statement on the Chinese Government's Web Site (http://english.gov.cn/2008-12/09/content_1172125.htm), in late 2008, China unveiled a four trillion yuan (US $586 billion) stimulus package and shifted its fiscal policy from a 「prudent」 to a 「proactive」 stance and eased monetary policy from 「tight」 to 「moderately loose」 to counter the global financial crisis. The financial stimulus package covers ten areas including: housing, rural infrastructure, transportation, health and education, environment, industry, disaster rebuilding, incomes, taxes, and finance. The central government ordered the stimulus plan to be implemented 「promptly」— the four trillion yuan had to be spent by 2010. After the plan was announced, officials from far and wide and from numerous departments lobbied the National Development and Reform Commission (NDRC) for a share of the package.

The *Asian Times* reported that the bulk of the government's investments, as well as bank loans, were going into the state sector. Close to 90% of the four trillion yuan that the State Council pumped into the economy in late 2008 has benefited SOEs rather than non-state sector firms. By contrast, some of the most active and efficient POEs (privately-owned enterprises) in the coastal provinces of Zhejiang and Guangdong have gone bankrupt due to such factors as failure to secure financing from state banks (source: http://www.atimes.com/atimes/China_Business/NA25Cb02.html).

Appendix 2

Yunnan Chihong Zinc & Germanium Co., Ltd:

The ownership structure of the company was highly concentrated. The share of the company held by the largest shareholder (51.32%) was 50 times that held by the second-largest shareholder (1.33%). The controlling shareholder of the company is the Yunye Group, which held more than 50% of the shares of Chihong for the past three years (except in the middle of 2006, when the percentage of shares held by the group fell to only 40%). The Yunye Group was a diversified enterprise. At the end of 2006, the percentage of Chihong's shares held by the Yunye Group reached 51.32%. Moreover, out of the nine directors in Chihong, five members of the board were from the Yunye Group.

According to the temporary announcements and regular reports from Chihong during the period December 31, 2006 to June 30, 2007, the company badly needed cash. The total amount of cash needed for the forthcoming programs would reach 700 million Yuan. Chihong's annual financial statement shows that, in 2006, the cash flow of each share from the company's operational activity was about 2.37 yuan. However, the cash dividend for each share during the same period was three yuan. This result indicates that Chihong's earnings in 2006 were far less than the cash dividends paid, not to mention the forthcoming programs. Chihong, however, still allotted a large amount of cash dividends, regardless of its serious shortage of cash.

Besides, on April 2, 2007, Chihong held a temporary board of directors meeting. The meeting approved a loan application for 600 million yuan from the bank. The loan was to be used as operational flow capital and for program construction. Coincidently, as the total capital stock of Chihong was 195 million shares, and for each 10 shares, a cash dividend of 30 yuan would be paid to the shareholders, a total of 585 million yuan cash would be needed, an amount close to the total amount of the loan applied.

國家圖書館出版品預行編目(CIP)資料

公司治理結構與治理機制研究：基於金融危機、股權分置改革的視角 / 劉春燕、內田交謹 著. -- 第一版.
-- 臺北市：財經錢線文化出版：崧博發行, 2018.11
　　面；　公分

ISBN 978-957-680-273-7(平裝)

1. 公司 2. 企業管理

553.97　　　　107018837

書　名：公司治理結構與治理機制研究：基於金融危機、股權分置改革的視角
作　者：劉春燕、內田交謹
發行人：黃振庭
出版者：財經錢線文化事業有限公司
發行者：崧博出版事業有限公司
E-mail：sonbookservice@gmail.com
粉絲頁　　　　　網　址：
地　址：台北市中正區延平南路六十一號五樓一室
8F.-815, No.61, Sec. 1, Chongqing S. Rd., Zhongzheng Dist., Taipei City 100, Taiwan (R.O.C.)
電　話：(02)2370-3310　傳　真：(02) 2370-3210
總經銷：紅螞蟻圖書有限公司
地　址：台北市內湖區舊宗路二段 121 巷 19 號
電　話：02-2795-3656　傳真：02-2795-4100　網址：
印　刷：京峯彩色印刷有限公司（京峰數位）

　　本書版權為西南財經大學出版社所有授權崧博出版事業有限公司獨家發行電子書及繁體書繁體版。若有其他相關權利及授權需求請與本公司聯繫。

定價：300元
發行日期：2018 年 11 月第一版
◎ 本書以POD印製發行